DEVOURING FREEDOM

CAN BIG GOVERNMENT EVER BE STOPPED?

W. JAMES ANTLE III

Editor, Daily Caller News Foundation

Since 1947
REGNERY
PUBLISHING, INC.
An Eagle Publishing Company • Washington, DC

Cataloging-in-Publication data on file with the Library of Congress
ISBN 978-1-62157-052-3

Published in the United States by

Regnery Publishing, Inc.
One Massachusetts Avenue NW
Washington, DC 20001

www.Regnery.com

Manufactured in the United States of America
10 9 8 7 6 5 4 3 2 1

Books are available in quantity for promotional or premium use. Write to Director of Special Sales, Regnery Publishing, Inc., One Massachusetts Avenue NW, Washington, DC 20001, for information on discounts and terms, or call (202) 216-0600.

Distributed to the trade by

Perseus Distribution
250 West 57th Street
New York, NY 10107

DEVOURING
FREEDOM

*To my grandmother Eleanor Grimes and in memory
of my grandparents William and Anna Antle*

CONTENTS

INTRODUCTION

I t seems like a century ago, but only seventeen years have passed. In 1996, a Democratic president stood before both houses of Congress and proclaimed, "The era of big government is over." Within the lifetime of a high school student, there was a bipartisan consensus that this country's problems could not be solved by an ever bigger, more expensive, and more intrusive federal government.

The forty-second president of the United States is not remembered for the accuracy of his public pronouncements, and this occasion proved to be no exception. Despite Bill Clinton's assurances, the era of big government was not over. The beast was just hibernating, forced into a cave when American voters tired of its attacks. But soon it would come roaring back into our lives.

For the first two hundred years of the Republic, from the presidencies of George Washington to Ronald Reagan, our annual federal budget was less than $1 trillion. The budget finally crossed the trillion-dollar threshold in 1987—under Reagan, alas (even Homer nods). It only took another fifteen years for the budget to reach $2 trillion annually, and then just another five to exceed $3 trillion.

Even without adjusting the numbers for inflation, that's an amazing trajectory. What it took two centuries for the federal government to spend, it can now outstrip easily in five years. The famous quip about government spending attributed to former Senate Republican leader Everett Dirksen—"A billion here, a billion there, and pretty soon you're talking real money"—would have to be updated to trillions.

Today, just the federal budget deficit—the difference between what Washington spends and what it collects in revenue each year—regularly exceeds $1 trillion. The Treasury Department recently announced that the nation is on course to run its fifth straight trillion-dollar deficit in 2013. The red ink has totaled as much as $1.4 trillion in a single year—almost as much as the entire federal budget the year Clinton declared an end to the era of big government.

And that's just one figure that captures how much America's political class is borrowing from the likes of China for future generations to repay. The national debt is now bigger than the entire U.S. economy—103 percent of gross domestic product. The federal government's total unfunded liabilities exceed $84 trillion and are growing all the time.

Of course, the era of big government was never really over. Federal spending kept rising even as Clinton uttered those famous words. And the full statement contains an important qualification, which hinted at how Washington might reassert itself: "The era of big government is over, but we can't go back to a time when our citizens were just left to fend for themselves."

Sound familiar? The alternative to reckless government growth is some imagined state of social Darwinism that never existed—even though, for much of our history, a relatively limited federal government, subject to the Constitution's restraints, did.

As I write, many are claiming that big government has been vindicated at the ballot box. President Barack Obama has been reelected. In an election in which it once seemed possible for Republicans to retake the Senate, Democrats actually gained seats. The only remaining obstacle to the unified control of the federal government that the Democrats enjoyed during the first two years of Obama's presidency is the Republican-dominated House—which is already showing familiar signs of caving in.

The *New York Times*' Paul Krugman openly pines for tax rates in excess of 90 percent: "Yet in the 1950s incomes in the top bracket faced a marginal tax rate of… 91 percent, while taxes on corporate profits were twice as large, relative to national income, as in recent years."[1]

At least liberals have finally found something nice to say about the 1950s!

For many, these are discouraging times. You see, big government wasn't the only thing in hibernation. For a while, it appeared that Obama had awakened a sleeping giant: the American taxpayer, who was tired of footing the bill for the liberal social engineers' schemes and determined to save his children and grandchildren from crippling debt.

A billion here, a billion there, in chronic deficit spending had finally given way to real money. The federal government was telling us what light bulbs to use in our homes, how much water there could be in our toilets, what food we could put in our bodies, and which products we could buy.

The federal government had long abused its powers to regulate interstate commerce by reclassifying wholly intrastate commerce. Now the feds were claiming that mere existence, especially if manifested as a refusal to take part in the regulated health insurance market, was interstate commerce. Even Democratic-appointed federal judges were skeptical of that line of constitutional reasoning.

Even Clinton's yarns about a social Darwinian dystopia acknowledged mediating institutions between the individual and the state: "We will meet [challenges] by going forward as one America, by working together in our communities, our schools, our churches and synagogues, our workplaces across the entire spectrum of our civic life." Obama's vision of an all-providing government crowds out civil society, with government as the only means of collective action.

The Tea Party took its name from the revolutionary protest in Boston Harbor against British taxation, and, some say, from the acronym for "taxed enough already." But the Tea Party movement, unlike previous protests and tax revolts, wasn't about taxation alone.

Government borrowing, the rising national debt that former Indiana governor Mitch Daniels has called "the new Red Menace," and the erosion of personal responsibility also drove a new wave of activists, some of them never before interested in politics, to take to the streets in protest.

No longer were demonstrations just for the left (though it wasn't long before the unbathed progressives of Occupy Wall Street horned in on the fun). Tea Partiers dressed up in powdered wigs like the Founding Fathers. They recited lines from the Constitution and Declaration of Independence. They carried signs proclaiming, "Your mortgage is not my problem!"

Like CNBC's Frank Santelli channeling the classic film *Network* on the floor of the Chicago stock exchange, they were mad as hell and they weren't going to take it anymore. And for a few euphoric months, it seemed they wouldn't have to.

A Republican was elected to Ted Kennedy's old Senate seat in Massachusetts, pledging to be the forty-first vote against the federal takeover of health care that had been Kennedy's life's work. Months later, Tea Party challengers ousted incumbent Republicans who had voted for bank bailouts and borrowed stimulus funds. By November, this wave washed the Democratic majority out of the House and eroded its numbers in the Senate.

Before long, there was a committed limited-government caucus in the Senate: Jim DeMint of South Carolina, Mike Lee of Utah, Rand Paul of Kentucky. They had allies like Pat Toomey of Pennsylvania, Marco Rubio of Florida, and Ron Johnson of Wisconsin—many of them elected without the support or encouragement of their local Republican leaders.

Two years later, the Democrats had Ted Kennedy's Senate seat again. The Republican elected in the "Scott heard round the world" who vowed to stop Obamacare was defeated, first in his attempt to halt the Affordable Care Act and then in his bid for reelection. Several Tea Party freshmen lost their House seats. The Supreme Court upheld Obamacare, with a Republican-appointed chief justice providing the majority vote. Obama himself was reelected.

As soon as it looked like real change was possible, the status quo reasserted itself with a vengeance.

It's tempting to give up. But even the 2012 election results contained seeds of good news. Paul Ryan, the Republican vice presidential nominee, grabbed the "third rail of American politics" enthusiastically and with both hands. He authored a budget proposal that contained detailed reforms to reduce spending and reform

Medicare. It passed the Republican-controlled House. The GOP presidential nominee, the man who tapped Ryan to be his running mate, embraced it implicitly (and sometimes explicitly).

Not since 1964, when Republicans nominated Barry Goldwater for president, had a major party backed sweeping changes to entitlements. There is no evidence that Mitt Romney and Paul Ryan lost the election because of Medicare or entitlement reform. They won voters over the age of sixty-five by a margin of 56 percent to 44 percent. The ticket carried those nearing retirement, from ages forty-five to sixty-four, by 51 percent to 47 percent.

Even those numbers reflect voter preferences that were not necessarily tied to entitlements, such as older blacks who voted overwhelmingly to reelect the country's first African-American president. "Mediscare" tactics notwithstanding, 61 percent of whites over the age of sixty-five gave their votes to Romney-Ryan, as did 61 percent of those between the ages of forty-five and sixty-four.

The retirees of Florida weren't frightened by Democratic ads saying Romney and Ryan would turn Medicare into a "voucher," which they made sound like a dirty word. The Republicans won 58 percent of Floridian voters above the age of sixty-five. They carried every age group over forty. Connie Mack, the Republican Senate candidate who disavowed the Ryan budget and expressed opposition to the Medicare reforms in particular, lost every one of those age groups.

None of this was enough to win Florida's electoral votes, much less to prevail nationally and win the White House. But the votes of senior citizens have deterred Republicans from pursuing reforms to Medicare and Social Security—the real long-term drivers of the debt—for years. That finally may be changing.

Lost in the post-election, post-inaugural fog is some much-needed perspective: Obama's reelection victory of 51 percent to 47 percent is roughly the same as George W. Bush's margin of victory in 2004. Obama's winning margins in the battleground states were similarly small. Bush's majorities were gone within two years.

"I earned capital in the campaign, political capital, and now I intend to spend it," Bush asserted at the time. The investment turned out to be about as profitable as Solyndra, and within months the reelected incumbent was as politically bankrupt as Washington, D.C.

It didn't take just one election—or one party—to make this mess. The federal budget reached $1 trillion, then $2 trillion, and then $3 trillion under Republican presidents. Bush bailed out Wall Street and the automakers. Romney, the man Republicans nominated to run against Obama, laid the groundwork for Obamacare.

The country no longer toils under 91-percent tax rates, which even Republican administrations once accepted. Wartime federal spending that eclipsed 40 percent of the economy was cut back. Even the mighty New Deal coalition, a much more plausible permanent majority for big government than Obama's showing, finally fell apart.

Therefore, it will take more than one election to fix this mess. I intend to show how we got here and offer some suggestions as to how to get out. It won't be easy. Sometimes it will seem impossible. But like a parent yanking his child to safety at the last second before he dashes into the street, Divine Providence has pulled this nation back from the abyss before.

In a speech at the *American Spectator*'s annual dinner a week after Obama's reelection, Senator Tom Coburn of Oklahoma laid out some of the challenges ahead and compared our situation to that of Washington at Valley Forge:

> They were hungry, weary, and ill-equipped. The conditions were brutal: 2,500 men—about 10 percent of his

army—perished that winter. Washington didn't know how many would survive, and of those that did, he didn't know if enough would re-enlist to carry on the struggle. But Washington refused to give up. He chose to lead. He decided to take action. He wasn't content to just survive and keep warm. Braving the wind and cold, he drilled his men daily. He honed his tactics and forged an army in a crucible of adversity.[2]

Coburn concluded, "America is a nation—and an idea—that has cheated history many times in the past and can do so again."

There's no time like the present.

CHAPTER ONE

STATISM BY STEALTH

arack Obama didn't promise to build a bigger government when he ran for president in that hope-and-change year of 2008. No major party nominee ever does. Instead, Obama pledged to cut the deficit in half.

In a debate a month before the presidential election, John McCain tried to tally his Democratic opponent's spending proposals. Obama would have none of it. Without a hint of irony, he insisted, "Actually, I'm cutting more than I'm spending so that it will be a net spending cut."[1]

Obama confined his talk of tax increases to "asking the wealthiest Americans to pay a little more." (It was never explained what would happen if they politely refused.) But he preferred to emphasize tax cuts.

Obama vowed that he would cut taxes for 95 percent of Americans. No one earning less than $200,000 a year would pay a dime more in taxes. For families, the threshold was $250,000. Obama's campaign website promised "generous tax cuts for low- and middle-income seniors, homeowners, the uninsured, and families sending a child to college or looking to save and accumulate wealth."

There were calls "to eliminate the capital gains tax for small businesses," to cut corporate taxes "for firms that invest and create jobs in the United States," and for tax incentives for "investments in innovation." Obama went so far as to say he would promote lower taxes than prevailed while Ronald Reagan was president, reducing tax revenues to 18.2 percent of GDP.[2]

OBAMA THE TAX SLAYER

In Obama's world, it was the Republicans who wanted to raise most Americans' taxes. He hit McCain for allegedly taxing health care. "Senator McCain would pay for his plan, in part, by taxing your health care benefits for the first time in history," Obama told an audience in Newport News, Virginia. "And this tax would come out of your paycheck. But the new tax credit he is proposing? That wouldn't go to you. It would go directly to your insurance company—not your bank account."

Budget expert Peter Ferrara argued at the time that Obama was playing fast and loose with the truth. "Obama here is practicing one of the Rules for Radicals he learned from the works of the openly socialist revolutionary Saul Alinsky during Obama's community organizer days," he wrote. "There is no need to be truthful when you are fighting for social justice. Make wild charges against your opponent and let him be stuck trying to explain the confusing details."[3]

Obama repeated this tactic in 2012 with vigor. If you lived in any of the battleground states, you undoubtedly saw Obama campaign ads repeatedly asserting that Mitt Romney would raise taxes on middle-class families by an average of $2,000. The commercial relied on a study that concluded that a middle-class tax hike would be required if Romney kept his promise to offset rate cuts with fewer deductions and loopholes: "Because taxpayers above $200,000 as a group have received a net tax cut, revenue neutrality requires that taxpayers below $200,000—about 95 percent of the population—experience a tax increase."[4]

To recap, Obama told the voters in 2008 that he would cut taxes for most of them, reduce taxes as a share of the economy, and become a bigger tax-cutter than Reagan, while halving the deficit and achieving a net reduction in federal spending. Only "million-aires and billionaires," big oil companies, and folks who fly on private jets would pay more. It was the Republicans who wanted to raise taxes, a move Obama would rebuff.

Four years later, it was hard to pretend that Obama had kept those promises—but that didn't keep him from trying. In April 2011, he asked an audience in Reno, "How many people here know that not only did we cut your taxes when I first came into office, but back in December we just cut your taxes again?"

"Taxes are lower now than they have been in a generation," Obama continued. "Taxes are a lot lower now than they were under Ronald Reagan. They're lower than they were under Bill Clinton. They're lower than they were under George Bush, in many cases."

That June, Obama repeated this claim to a more skeptical audience—House Republicans who had come to the White House for debt-ceiling negotiations. The chairman of the House Oversight and Government Reform Committee, Darrell Issa, a Republican from California, told *The Hill* afterward, "We learned we had the lowest tax rates in history … lower than Reagan!"

After reports of Republican "eye-rolling," supporters of the president leapt to his defense. The Center for American Progress gloated on its blog, "GOP can't handle the truth: taxes lower under Obama than Reagan." (The posting on the "Think Progress" blog went on, incoherently, to condemn many of the tax cuts on which its analysis relied as "misguided." So is it a good thing taxes were so low in 2011 or not?)

Some nonpartisan fact-checkers also sided with the president. One cited the Tax Policy Center's report, "Historical Federal Income Tax Rates for a Family of Four." Looking at the average income tax rate on the median income for a family of four from 1955 through 2010, the group concluded, "The average income tax rate under Reagan in 1983 was 11.06 percent. Under Clinton in 1992, it was 9.18 percent. And under Obama in 2010, it was 4.68 percent." On this basis, the fact-checker vouched for Obama. "Truthmeter: 10," was one group's scientific verdict. But it would be more accurate to describe the president's tax claims as "partially true with some important context missing."

The fiscal stimulus contained a payroll tax credit of $116 billion for those earning less than $75,000. According to one estimate, this tax cut saved 97 percent of U.S. households an average of $1,179 in 2009. It was extended in 2010 and 2012, but allowed to lapse at the end of the year. But it was a temporary tax cut, and the Obama administration was willing to let it expire in a second term.

Another reason taxes were low? The Bush tax cuts, some of which the Obama administration was eager to kill. Without those tax cuts, the top tax rate isn't lower than what it was under Bill Clinton. And without those tax cuts, which Obama takes credit for agreeing to extend, taxes would not have been lowered for 80 percent of Americans.

Then there are the Reagan tax cuts, which eventually brought the top marginal tax rate all the way down to 28 percent. The top statutory rate was 70 percent when Reagan took office and began to cut taxes, part of the reason that tax rates were higher in 1983 than in 2010. But the top tax rate was lower when Reagan left office than it was at the end of Obama's first term.

To be sure, Obama has repeatedly advocated continuing the tax cuts for all but the higher income earners: individuals bringing in more than $200,000 annually and families earning more than $250,000. (He accepted a $400,000 threshold for individuals and $450,000 for families at the end of 2012.) But his position has repeatedly endangered the renewal of the tax cuts for the middle and working classes.

More importantly, Obama's spending commitments imply much larger tax increases that will eventually ensnare the middle class. If the federal government's $84 trillion in unfunded liabilities are not addressed, to cite just one example, taxes will have to rise by 30 percent.

So yes, Obama is a big tax-cutter, if you include tax cuts he has favored rescinding, tax cuts he is open to rescinding, and tax cuts that will ultimately be unsustainable if we continue on his path of government spending.

WHAT SPENDING INCREASES?

The president's claims about low tax rates during his first term at least have some factual basis, however distorted they are. But no one can deny the vast increases in government spending and deficits that have occurred on Obama's watch—*can* he?

As it turns out, he can. A widely circulated MarketWatch report claimed that Obama's binge never happened. "Of all the falsehoods told about President Barack Obama," opined Rex Nutting, "the biggest whopper is the one about his reckless spending spree." He went on to argue, "federal spending is rising at the slowest pace since Dwight Eisenhower brought the Korean War to an end in the 1950s."[5]

Less than a month before the election, the *Huffington Post* published an only slightly less ambitious manifesto: "Repeat after me: Obama cut the deficit and slowed spending to lowest level in 50 years." Concerning claims that Obama was an overspending president, its author wrote, "Pants on fire *times a thousand*" (emphasis his).

More recently, Jed Graham wrote in *Investor's Business Daily*, "Believe it or not, the federal deficit has fallen faster over the past three years than it has in any such stretch since demobilization from World War II." Though at least Graham acknowledged, "President Obama hasn't gotten much credit for reining in the deficit, probably because a big part of the deficit progress has come from the unwinding of extraordinary government supports that he helped put in place."

Even the president himself got into the act. "[F]ederal spending since I took office has risen at the slowest pace of any president in almost sixty years,"[6] Obama boasted at a campaign rally in Des Moines, Iowa. White House press secretary Jay Carney attributed reports of the administration's fiscal follies to "sloth and laziness."[7]

Obama was more pointed about it at a campaign event in Denver, Colorado. "I'd just point out that [spending] always goes up least under Democratic presidents," he said. "This other side, I don't know how they've been bamboozling folks into thinking that they are the responsible, fiscally disciplined party. They run up these wild debts, and then when we take over, we've got to clean it up. And they point and say, look how irresponsible they are. Look at the facts. Look at the numbers."[8]

This was too much even for the mainstream media fact-checkers. Consider this reaction from the Associated Press: "Obama rests his claim on an analysis by MarketWatch.... The analysis simply looks at the year-to-year topline spending number for the government but doesn't account for distortions baked into the figures by the Wall Street bailout and government takeover of the mortgage lending giants Fannie Mae and Freddie Mac."[9]

Evaluating the argument that Obama is responsible for spending growth of only 1.4 percent between 2010 and 2013, the AP fact-checker notes, "Those are stunningly low figures considering that Obama rammed through Congress an $831 billion stimulus measure in early 2009 and presided over significant increases in annual spending by domestic agencies at the same time the cost of benefit programs like Social Security, Medicare, and Medicaid were ticking steadily higher."

Then there is the matter of the Wall Street bailout known as the Troubled Asset Relief Program. The money was largely paid out in 2009 and the banks and Wall Street firms began paying it back in 2010. Obama defenders misleadingly count this as a spending cut by the administration. They engage in a similar sleight of hand regarding the federal bailouts of Fannie Mae and Freddie Mac, using the fact that most of the takeovers occurred in 2009 rather than 2010 to conjure up a phantom spending cut.

"Taken together, TARP and the takeover of Fannie and Freddie combine to give Obama an undeserved $317 billion swing in the 2010 figures and the resulting 1.8 percent cut from 2009," the AP fact-checker concluded. "A fairer reading is an almost 8 percent increase."

Washington Post fact-checker Glenn Kessler gave Obama's claims of frugality "three Pinocchios."[10] Kessler noted that anyone making such arguments gives Obama less responsibility for 2009 spending than he really deserves and "gives Obama credit for automatic spending cuts that he wants to halt."

"In theory, one could claim that the budget was already locked in when Obama took office, but that's not really the case," Kessler wrote. "Most of the appropriations bills had not been passed, and certainly the stimulus bill was only signed into law after Obama took office." And when you look at the Congressional Budget Office's analysis of the president's proposed budgets, he actually requested more money than Congress agreed to spend.

The huge spending and deficit reduction totals touted in the *Huffington Post*, meanwhile, are possible only because there were such large increases in the first place. In other words, only by starting so high can Obama go so low. In trying to give the president credit for $500 billion in deficit reduction, for example, the author actually boasts, "the CBO projected that the 2013 Obama budget, if enacted as is, would shrink the deficit to $977 billion."

Only $977 billion, a figure larger than the 1986 federal budget! For most Americans, locking in the post-stimulus spending levels and deficits in the range of $1 trillion a year doesn't count as fiscal discipline.

Obama has been confronted with these arguments before. In January 2010, he met with House Republicans in Baltimore. Two days earlier, he proposed freezing non-security-related discretionary spending in his State of the Union address. It was not the "flexible freeze" that President George H. W. Bush once called for—would you want to skate on a flexibly frozen river? But it contained some budget gimmickry to make it work.

The GOP was still in the minority in the House at the time and was without any meaningful leverage in the legislative negotiations. But a Wisconsin Republican by the name of Paul Ryan decided to challenge the president anyway.

"I serve as a ranking member of the Budget Committee, so I'm going to talk a little budget if you don't mind," Ryan said. "The spending bills that you've signed into law, the domestic discretionary spending has been increased by 84 percent. You now want to freeze spending at this elevated level beginning next year. This means that total spending in your budget would grow at three-hundredths of 1 percent less than otherwise. I would simply submit that we could do more and start now."

Obama replied that he wanted to "just push back a little bit on the underlying premise about us increasing spending by 84 percent." Showing the assertiveness that has been known to send a thrill up Chris Matthews's leg, Obama averred, "The fact of the matter is, is that most of the increases in this year's budget, this past year's budget, were not as a consequence of policies that we initiated but instead were built in as a consequence of the automatic stabilizers that kick in because of this enormous recession."

"Automatic stabilizers" are increases in means-tested entitlement programs that are triggered by economic downturns, as poverty and joblessness cause more people to qualify for more benefits under the law.

Ryan wasn't fooled. "I would simply say that automatic stabilizer spending is mandatory spending," he replied. "The discretionary spending, the bills that Congress signs that you sign into law, that has increased 84 percent." In what the journalist Philip Klein described as a "tacit acknowledgement that he had been bested," Obama retreated lamely, "We'll have a longer debate on the budget numbers, all right?"[11]

The president then moved on to the next question.

NOT SO NEW DEAL

Obama's bait-and-switch tactic is nothing new. Franklin D. Roosevelt ushered in the New Deal and was the architect of the modern American welfare state. Seeking his first presidential term in 1932, he posed as a deficit hawk.

Roosevelt promised to balance the budget. Speaking at Forbes Field in Pittsburgh a month before the election, he railed against Republican president Herbert Hoover's "wasteful and extravagant spending" and unprecedented peacetime deficits. While these charges cut against Hoover's reputation as a tightfisted chief executive who treated nickels like manhole covers, Roosevelt had a point.

Under Hoover, a $700 million surplus was turned into a $2.6 billion deficit. That doesn't sound like much, but keep in mind that the federal government spent only $4.6 billion total in 1932. Economist Robert Murphy writes, "as a percentage of the overall budget, the 1932 deficit was astounding—it would translate into a *$3.3 trillion* deficit in 2007 (instead of the actual deficit of $162 billion that year)."[12]

It would nevertheless seem trivial compared to the deficit spending and government growth that followed in FDR's four terms as president. As Kenneth T. Walsh has observed in *U.S. News & World Report*, "It didn't take long for FDR to jettison one of his major campaign promises—to balance the budget." Roosevelt "felt the pledge was outweighed by the need for government activism, and he began a new era of vast deficit spending."[13]

The journalist William White wrote approvingly that FDR's election revealed "a firm desire on the part of the American people to use government as an agency for human welfare." That's one way of describing it. As Walsh put it, "The electorate had, in effect, taken nearly 150 years of tradition upholding limited government and, in their anxiety and anger, thrown it out the window."

Roosevelt exceeded Hoover's annual deficits only twice. But the national debt ballooned from $22.5 billion at the start of his presidency to $258.5 billion when he died in office in 1945. More strikingly, federal spending zoomed from 3.4 percent of GDP in 1930 to

12 percent in 1941. By the time FDR died in 1945, federal spending was 43.6 percent of the economy.

Much of the later increase was due to fighting World War II. Once the Axis was defeated and the war was won, Washington's share of the national economy subsided. But the growth in federal spending that was a result of the welfare state proved more enduring. Federal spending as a percentage of GDP would never again fall into the single digits, where it was for most of the nation's pre-New Deal history, and it would drop below 12 percent only once more, in 1948.

After Roosevelt's presidency, a strong centralized government rather than a decentralized federal republic became the norm. So did a large federal role in the economy and chronic budget deficits. Many Americans—and most economists—came to embrace the radical idea that deficits enhance, rather than detract from, prosperity. What the country wanted from Washington, and what Washington could take from the people, changed dramatically.

Yet even the most vocal proponents of big government liberalism still try to persuade the American people that they can maintain an activist federal government at a low cost to taxpayers and with little waste. FDR promised balanced budgets, Obama smaller deficits. The country's political consciousness is uneasily divided between fiscal conservatism and belief in limited government on the one hand and the acceptance of the swollen post-New Deal state on the other.

Before he was elected, Obama said he wanted to be a transformational president. While the parallels with FDR are obvious, Obama himself cited a comparison that struck most political reporters as odd: "I think Ronald Reagan changed the trajectory of America in a way that Richard Nixon did not, and a way that Bill Clinton did not," Obama said. Reagan spoke to a country that was saying, "We want clarity, we want optimism, we want a return to that sense of dynamism and entrepreneurship that had been missing."[14]

The remark enraged Clintonites and Reaganites alike, albeit for different reasons. In some ways, it's not so odd. Reagan himself voted for FDR four times before drifting toward the Republicans during the Eisenhower administration and ultimately joining the party in 1962. For his part, he never saw any contradiction between his past as a New Deal Democrat and his record as a politician who was trying to restore the ideal of limited government that Roosevelt's revolution overthrew.

LIBERAL REAGAN OR ROOSEVELT REDUX?

Obama's aspiration to be the "liberal Reagan," as Andrew Sullivan has described him, has less to do with Reagan's policies than with his transformational influence. The Tea Party movement was started when grassroots conservatives feared that Obama was succeeding.

There is something to this idea. Obama has embarked on a path that will change the citizen's relationship with his government, a path that will restructure the economy in ways that make free enterprise less important and government cronyism more important. But at the same time he is merely confirming a trend in American politics that Reagan tried to halt and reverse.

The upward trajectory in federal spending is one such trend. In his first term, Obama presided over the start of three fiscal years. Journalist Terence Jeffrey notes, "these are three of the only four fiscal years since the Japanese surrendered on September 2, 1945, that the federal government has spent more than 24 percent of GDP."[15]

"The fourth fiscal year since the end of World War II in which the federal government spent more than 24 percent of GDP was 2009," Jeffrey continued. "That fiscal year started when George W. Bush was president and ended when Obama was president." That would be the year of the $700 billion bank bailout, which Obama supported, and the $831 billion stimulus package, which he proposed and signed into law.

And then there is the debt. In less than four years under Obama, the federal government borrowed more money than it had from George Washington's presidency to early in George W. Bush's first term. By one estimate, the national debt now stands at $49,568 per household.

Around the time these numbers were being reported, Treasury Secretary Timothy Geithner called for empowering Obama to raise the debt ceiling unilaterally.

"He said that Congress could be allowed to pass a resolution blocking an increase in the debt limit, but that the president would be able to veto that resolution," the *New York Times* reported. "Only if two-thirds of lawmakers overrode that veto could Congress block a higher borrowing limit."[16]

Joseph Weisenthal of *Business Insider*, an unrepentant Keynesian, described Geithner's proposal as "so reasonable, nobody could possibly disagree."[17]

No, thanks.

When forced to address the country's fiscal disarray, the Obama administration's response has been to propose large tax increases and phantom spending cuts. The president calls this a "balanced approach." Many observers find it a bit off-balance.

Senate Minority Leader Mitch McConnell said he "burst into laughter" when Geithner briefed him on Obama's proposal.[18] But for future generations of Americans saddled with debt, the outcome isn't likely to be so funny.

Government is getting bigger and more expensive under Obama. The question is whether his elevated levels of spending will become the "new normal" in America. Despite the confident assurances of those selling a "permanent Democratic majority," that's not a question that was answered by the 2012 election or by Obama's return to the White House for a second term. The definitive answer will come over the next four years and beyond.

After congratulating his record on spending at that exuberant rally in Denver, the president made his closing pitch. "And now, I want to finish the job," said Obama. "I want to finish the job in a balanced way. Yes, we're going to streamline government. There's more waste to be cut."

Even the biggest booster of big government, in the midst of asking for another four years in office, did not emphasize the spending he would increase or the taxes he would raise. He did not lead with an impassioned defense of Obamacare.

Obama instead offered to finish imposing fiscal discipline and keep streamlining government. "There's more waste to be cut." The sales pitch may have been disingenuous, but it was made for a good reason.

CHAPTER TWO

THE GOVERNMENT
WE DON'T DESERVE

Most Americans instinctively dislike big government. That may seem hard to believe given some recent election results, but those who have studied public attitudes about the size of government have consistently found it to be true.

Don't just take the pollsters' word for it. Why else do big-government politicians running outside of safely liberal districts pretend to be anything but big-government politicians? Franklin D. Roosevelt promised to balance the budget, Jimmy Carter called for "zero-based budgeting," Bill Clinton declared that the era of big government was over, and Barack Obama insisted that he wanted a net federal spending cut. George W. Bush, the nominally Republican president who outspent Clinton, remarked in August 2001,

"One of my jobs as President is to make sure we keep fiscal sanity in the budget."[1]

But there are dirty jobs American politicians just won't do, and keeping "fiscal sanity in the budget" is one of them.

NOBODY LOVES BIG GOVERNMENT

While survey results can tell you only so much, it's nevertheless instructive to look at the public opinion data on people's preferences for smaller or larger government. The polling expert Karlyn Bowman examined *New York Times*–CBS News and *Washington Post*–ABC News polls on this question from the mid-1970s to the middle of the last decade. The percentage of people who preferred smaller government increased over that period from a low of 44 percent in 1976 to a high of 64 percent in 2004. The preference for larger government fell from a high of 41 percent to a low of 22 percent.

When the Pew Research Center asked registered voters in September 2012 whether they preferred a "smaller government with fewer services" or a "bigger government providing more services," they chose smaller government by 56 percent to 35 percent. A Fox News poll taken around the same time found that 51 percent wanted smaller government and 41 percent wanted bigger government.

What happens when polls include a question about the higher taxes that would accompany additional government services? In May 2012, Rasmussen Reports asked likely voters whether they prefer a government with fewer services and lower taxes to one with more services and higher taxes. Fewer services and lower taxes beat more services and higher taxes by 64 percent to 25 percent, with 11 percent undecided.

Rasmussen reported, "That's unchanged from last month and consistent with findings in regular surveys since late 2006." And it's not just Republicans who feel this way. The *Washington Post* and the Kaiser Family Foundation looked at the slice of independent voters who were truly uncommitted to either party—many self-described independents are really partisans in their voting behavior who just don't want to own the label—yet politically engaged.

They found that among this 5-percent slice of the electorate—bigger than the winning margin in the 2012 presidential contest—64 percent want a smaller government with fewer services while only 32 percent want to increase federal spending to create jobs. Just 26 percent have a favorable view of Obamacare.

Big government supporters were in the minority even among those who turned out in the November 2012 presidential election. According to exit polls, 51 percent of voters said that government is doing too many things better left to businesses and individuals, while only 43 percent believed that government needs to do more to solve problems.

But advocates of big government were more united. Four-fifths of those who told exit pollsters they wanted the government to do more voted to reelect Barack Obama. Only three-fourths of those who thought the government was doing too much cast their ballots for Mitt Romney.

Nevertheless, remember these results the next time someone says Obama's reelection was a mandate for big government.

OBAMA'S BIG-GOVERNMENT BRUISES

If anything, Obama's embrace of big government hurt him politically, at least for the first two years of his presidency. A 2011 *Washington Post*–ABC News poll found that, while 56 percent of Americans said they wanted smaller government, 70 percent correctly answered that their president favored bigger government.

Only 18 percent—less than one in five—thought Obama wanted smaller government, despite his boasts of being the most tightfisted president since Eisenhower.

A little over a year into Obama's administration, the reporter Dan Balz noted the discrepancy between the president's statist initiatives and a similar *Post* poll showing voter preference for smaller government:

> The poll also shows how much ground Obama has lost during his first year of trying to convince the public that more government is the answer to the country's problems. By 58 percent to 38 percent, Americans said they prefer smaller government and fewer services to larger government with more services. Since he won the Democratic nomination in June 2008, the margin between those favoring smaller over larger government has moved in *Post*-ABC polls from five points to 20 points.[2]

Obama hasn't moved public opinion on Washington's power and cost, even as he has worked to increase dependency on government by increasing its size.

WHOM DO YOU TRUST?

Gallup takes the public's pulse on the size of government by asking a different question: "In your opinion, which of the following will be the biggest threat to the country in the future: big business, big labor, or big government?"

Majorities have considered big government the biggest threat for years. In December 2011, the date of the most recent poll on this subject, 64 percent of respondents identified big government as the biggest threat—just one point shy of the record high. Only 26 percent named big business, while a mere 8 percent named big labor.

Despite public skepticism of large corporations, big business has never been identified as the biggest threat by more than 38 percent of the respondents, and that was at the height of the Enron scandal in 2002. Almost half of Democrats say big government is the biggest threat, beating out big business by four percentage points. Fully 64 percent of independents and 82 percent of Republicans agree. Distrust of government has risen enormously since the heyday of the Great Society in 1965, the first year Gallup asked the question, when only 35 percent deemed big government the biggest threat.

When asked directly, the American people don't want the federal government to get bigger. They would rather get by with fewer government services than pay more in taxes.

SMALL-GOVERNMENT VOTES, BIG-GOVERNMENT VICTORIES

So why does the federal government keep getting bigger? Why do the same people who say they don't trust the government or want it to be smaller turn around and vote for politicians who will make government bigger?

It's not that they don't know their votes will lead to more government. An August 2012 *Washington Post*–ABC News poll found that 59 percent of respondents wanted a smaller government while 73 percent believed Obama would make government bigger. Yet the survey showed voters split on whom they preferred for president, and Obama ended up winning a bare majority of the popular vote on Election Day.

One problem is that many voters don't understand where federal spending is going. That makes it easier for demagogic politicians to

pretend to be cutting large programs when they are proposing min-
iscule spending cuts. They can similarly portray budget-busting
spending as fiscally sound.

In a time of record deficits, it might be a good idea to cut back
on foreign aid or subsidies for public broadcasting. (I would argue
that such cuts *are* a good idea.) But they won't save very much
money. A 2011 CNN–Opinion Research Corporation poll tested voters' budget IQs. The results showed that Americans on average
believe that foreign aid constitutes 10 percent of the federal budget.
One in five thinks the figure is closer to 30 percent. Some 60 percent
say they back cuts in foreign aid, which is all to the good—but in
2010, the last budget before the poll was taken, international assis-
tance accounted for just 1 percent of the $3.5 trillion the federal
government spent.

Mitt Romney may have gotten into hot water with some voters
for saying he would take a budget axe to Big Bird during the presidential debates, but CNN found that about half of those polled back
major cuts to the Corporation for Public Broadcasting. They estimate that public television and radio account for about 5 percent
of the budget, while the reality is closer to one-tenth of 1 percent.

This episode is brought to you by the number "trillion."

Many state governments are financially crippled by unfunded
pension benefits promised to public employees. The severity of this
crisis contributed to Governor Scott Walker's victory in the Wisconsin recall election. But government workers aren't as large a driver
of fiscal problems at the federal level. While poll respondents estimate that 10 percent of the federal budget goes to employees' pensions and retirement benefits, the actual figure is closer to 3.5
percent.

"Firing every federal government employee," writes the author
David Wessel, "wouldn't save enough to even cut the deficit in half."[3]

About a third of respondents in the CNN poll back defense spending cuts, but they wrongly assume that the Pentagon is responsible for 30 percent of the federal budget. The truth is that by 2010, military spending had already tumbled to 19 percent of the budget. The growth of entitlements and interest on the national debt threaten to further shrink the military's share.

"The public has a better idea of how much the government spends on programs like Social Security and Medicare, but there is a related problem—cutting them has little public support," said CNN's polling director, Keating Holland. "The result: cutting unpopular programs would probably not cut the deficit very much, and cutting the deficit would probably require cuts in programs that Americans like."[4]

"GET THE GOVERNMENT OUT OF MY MEDICARE"

There's a (possibly apocryphal) story that dates back to Bill and Hillary Clinton's attempted federal takeover of health care. At the height of the Hillarycare debate in 1994, Capitol Hill fax and phone lines were jammed with communications from concerned voters. Most Americans did not want Clinton's scheme to become law. Much to the surprise of many Democrats, who had assumed retirees would be a powerful constituency for national health insurance, senior citizens heavily opposed the legislation. "Get the government out of my Medicare," one old lady supposedly protested. A caricature was born.

Years later, the image resurfaced in the Obamacare debate. An angry old man appeared at a town hall meeting hosted by Rep. Bob Inglis, a Republican from South Carolina, and reportedly said, "Keep your government hands off my Medicare." "I had to politely explain that, 'Actually, sir, your health care is being provided by the government,'" Inglis subsequently told the *Washington Post*. "But he wasn't having any of it."

The president also reported hearing this objection to Obamacare. "I got a letter the other day from a woman," Obama began. "She said, 'I don't want government-run health care. I don't want socialized medicine. And don't touch my Medicare.'"[5]

Cue liberal laugh track here. These tales are told to suggest that opposition to big government in general, and government-run health care in particular, is rooted in ignorance and hypocrisy. The liberal blogger Bob Cesca offered this death-panel diagnosis for senior citizens protesting Obamacare at town hall meetings. "They're participating in a corporate lobbyist–driven campaign to prevent the rest of us from acquiring the same affordable, reliable public health care they enjoy," he wrote. "In other words, their government-run health care is excellent. So excellent that it can't be shared."[6]

In the same post, Cesca sang the praises of the "amazing" U.S. postal service, suggesting that his view of excellence might be somewhat skewed. At least he is probably a cheap date.

But there *is* a degree of selectiveness about people's opposition to big government. Even many conservatives are reluctant to champion lower spending on entitlement programs that benefit either the elderly or the middle class. A 2011 Marist poll found that self-described Tea Party supporters opposed "major cuts" to Social Security and Medicare by a 76-percent to 22-percent margin. A *Wall Street Journal*–NBC News poll found that Tea Partiers by a two-to-one margin considered significant cuts to Social Security "unacceptable."

A *New York Times*–CBS News poll found that Tea Party supporters were as likely as other voters to believe Social Security and Medicare were worth their cost to taxpayers. "That's a conundrum, isn't it?" the *Times* quoted sixty-two-year-old Jodine White as saying. "I don't know what to say. Maybe I don't want smaller government. I guess I want smaller government and my Social Security. I didn't look at it from the perspective of losing things I need. I think I've changed my mind."[7]

Other reputable polls have produced different results, and outcomes vary greatly based on how the questions are asked. But White's "conundrum" is nothing new, nor is it unique to a particular *New York Times* story. The Republican Party, and, to a lesser extent, the conservative movement have a history of opposing welfare except when it is welfare for farmers, businesses, churches, or old people—all important Republican voting blocs. A lot of people want smaller government and their Social Security.

Of course, Social Security and Medicare were designed as "earned entitlements" for this very reason. People pay into the system and are told they own their benefits. Never mind that the Social Security trust fund is an accounting fiction, that payroll taxes actually fund current beneficiaries rather than some future nest egg, and that these programs resemble a Ponzi scheme more than an insurance plan. The Supreme Court has ruled that Social Security benefits are not a contractual right.

At a time when two-thirds of Americans pay more in payroll taxes to fund entitlements than they pay in income taxes, people justly feel that they have paid into the system and therefore deserve to collect. It is their money.

"NO DAMN POLITICIAN"

Franklin Roosevelt explicitly sought to prevent Social Security from being funded by general revenues for fear that, if it looked like a welfare program, it would be politically vulnerable. Roosevelt recalled in 1941, "We put those payroll contributions there so as to give the contributors a legal, moral, and political right to collect their pensions.... With those taxes in there, no damn politician can ever scrap my Social Security program."[8]

One conservative columnist observed of Roosevelt's boast, "He was right. It has proved much more difficult to repeal Social Security than to repeal inconvenient parts of the U.S. Constitution." Medicare was similarly structured.

Democratic attack ads notwithstanding, almost no one wants to repeal Social Security or Medicare. But changes need to be made to both programs to make them solvent and to alleviate the metastasizing national debt crisis.

Reform is also necessary to contain big government. We have reached the point where more than two-thirds of the federal budget simply grows automatically, without any vote of Congress. Social Security and Medicare are two big reasons for this development.

BENEFITS GOOD, TAXES BAD

Selective anti-statism hurts efforts to curtail big government, but it's not as if there is no hypocrisy on the other side. Consider the case of Susan Estrich, the lawyer and liberal activist who managed Michael Dukakis's 1988 presidential campaign and now writes a nationally syndicated newspaper column. After the 2012 presidential election, Estrich catalogued the reasons she had cast her ballot for Obama. "I voted for him because I know how hard it is to buy health insurance for a single person with even a minor pre-existing condition," she wrote. "I voted for Obama because I worry about cutting back on environmental regulation."

"I voted for Obama because I believe local schools need help from the federal government," Estrich continued, "because I believe we are one country, and that if there is an earthquake in California, we will need as much help from our fellow states—which is to say the federal government—as New York and New Jersey do in dealing with the aftermath of Hurricane Sandy."

She continued in this vein, until her paean screeched to an abrupt halt. "I did not vote for Obama because I think I am paying too little in taxes," she concluded.[9]

Come again?

"Like many people I know, I am 'rich' by Obama's standards," Estrich argued. "I pay more taxes, percentage wise, than Mitt Romney and Warren Buffett, because I earn virtually every penny of my income."

Susan Estrich *did* build that.

"I am all for closing loopholes," she went on. "I am all for ending deductions for things I don't even understand. But I am not for putting a low cap on deductions that would make it all but impossible for the charities I support to raise funds."

Estrich went on to warn Obama that she didn't think she was alone, and that he was not reelected to raise taxes. (Obama may agree, at least based on some of the things he said during the campaign about taxes for the 95 percent.) Estrich's column could be boiled down to this: government benefits are great, but don't tax me to pay for them.

This viewpoint is widely shared. Warren Buffett, the fantastically wealthy investor, earns media plaudits for saying that the rich should pay more in taxes. But Gregory Mankiw, chairman of the economics department at Harvard University, pointed out that Buffett doesn't call for closing the tax loopholes he actually benefits from:

1. His company Berkshire Hathaway never pays a dividend but instead retains all earnings. So the return on this

investment is entirely in the form of capital gains. By not paying dividends, he saves his investors (including himself) from having to immediately pay income tax on this income.

2. Mr. Buffett is a long-term investor, so he rarely sells and realizes a capital gain. His unrealized capital gains are untaxed.

3. He is giving away much of his wealth to charity. He gets a deduction at the full market value of the stock he donates, most of which is unrealized (and therefore untaxed) capital gains.

4. When he dies, his heirs will get a stepped-up basis. The income tax will never collect any revenue from the substantial unrealized capital gains he has been accumulating.[10]

Yes, even Warren Buffett is a firm believer in the adage about taxation attributed to Senator Russell Long: "Don't tax you, don't tax me, tax that fellow behind the tree."

THE "47 PERCENT"

Mitt Romney was caught on tape. That's a problem that few predicted at the outset of the 2012 presidential campaign. The strait-laced Republican presidential candidate doesn't drink coffee or Coke, much less alcohol. He is more *I Love Lucy* than *The Hangover*. It didn't seem terribly likely he would be captured on video doing anything particularly scandalous.

Yet during the fall campaign, a Romney video did surface. It wasn't salacious, like a Hollywood celebrity sex tape, but it created a major controversy nonetheless. Romney was clandestinely taped talking to some high-dollar donors. The venue was a $50,000-a-plate dinner in Boca Raton, Florida. The left-wing magazine *Mother Jones* obtained the footage.

"There are 47 percent of the people who will vote for the president no matter what," Romney began. "All right, there are 47 percent who are with him, who are dependent upon government, who believe that they are victims, who believe the government has a responsibility to care for them, who believe that they are entitled to health care, to food, to housing, to you-name-it. That that's an entitlement. And the government should give it to them. And they will vote for this president no matter what."

"Forty-seven percent of Americans pay no income taxes," Romney continued. "So our message of tax cuts doesn't connect. He'll be out there talking about tax cuts for the rich. I mean, that's what they sell every four years."[11]

The conclusion Romney drew may be what did the most political damage: "So my job is not to worry about those people, I'll never convince them they should take personal responsibility and care for their lives. What I have to do is convince the 5 to 10 percent in the center that are independents that are thoughtful, that look at voting one way or the other depending upon in some cases emotion, whether they like the guy or not, what he looks like."

The Romney campaign later disavowed the statements as inelegant phrasing, but his running mate, Paul Ryan, also spoke of the "makers versus the takers." Campaigning in New Hampshire, Ryan observed, "We risk hitting a tipping point in our society where we have more takers than makers in society, where we will have turned our safety net into a hammock that lulls able-bodied people into lives of dependency and complacency." He said Obama's policies were "feverishly putting more people into the column of being takers than makers, of being more dependent."

Unlike Romney, Ryan did not put a number on those who were dependent on government—he had previously said that 30 percent backed the welfare state while 70 percent preferred an "opportunity society"—but in the past he had worried about welfare state clients becoming a majority. "We're coming close to a tipping point in America, where we might have a net majority of takers versus makers in society," he said. "And that could become very dangerous if it sets in as a permanent condition."[12]

After losing the presidential election to Obama, Romney triggered speculation that this tipping point had arrived. It was another leaked conference with donors—this time a campaign postmortem on why he had failed to unseat the president.

"What... the president's campaign did was focus on certain members of his base coalition, give them extraordinary financial gifts from the government, and then work very aggressively to turn them out to vote, and that strategy worked," Romney told them. "I mean it's a proven political strategy, which is give a bunch of money from the government to a—to a group and, guess what, they'll vote for you."

Romney enumerated some of the benefits promised to young people, women, and minorities in explaining why he had such a hard time breaking through to those voting blocs ("especially the African-American community, the Hispanic community, and young people"). He said a future Democratic candidate will probably run on expanding Obamacare to include free dental care. He concluded, "the giving away free stuff... is a hard thing to compete with."

With the White House no longer on the line, many prominent Republicans denounced Romney's comments. "I don't think it's helpful," said Iowa governor Terry Branstad. "I guess my feeling is that we need to turn the page, and we need to focus on the future and not make excuses for the past."[13]

Governor Chris Christie of New Jersey said, "You can't expect to be a leader of all the people and be divisive." He opined that Romney made his remarks because he was "very upset" and "very disappointed."[14]

"I don't want to rebut him point by point," said Senator Marco Rubio of Florida. "I would just say to you, I don't believe that we have millions and millions of people in this country that don't want to work."[15]

Governor Bobby Jindal of Louisiana said, "I absolutely reject that notion, that description. I think that's absolutely wrong." He went on to suggest that Romney's comments "don't represent where we are as a party or where we're going as a party."[16] Jindal later took to Twitter to say that voters won't like a candidate if they don't think he likes them.

The former governor of Minnesota Tim Pawlenty told C-SPAN, "You know, I don't think it's as simple as saying the president gave out gifts. I just don't think it's that simple. There's a lot more to it than that." Pawlenty said he thought voters decided which candidate "they prefer because of leadership considerations and also [who they think] can understand their needs the best."

Former Speaker of the House Newt Gingrich thundered, "I just think it's nuts. I mean, first of all, it's insulting." Gingrich and Pawlenty were Romney's rivals for the Republican presidential nomination in 2012. Christie, Rubio, and Jindal are possible candidates in 2016.

The columnist George Will concluded simply, "Quit despising the American people."

Strangely enough, Romney ended up winning 47 percent of the popular vote.

Undoubtedly, there were some problems with Romney's analysis, both in the conference call and in Boca Raton. First was his emphasis on the people who don't pay income taxes, which is not an accurate measure of government dependency.

Many Americans have stopped paying taxes because of Republican tax cuts. When Ronald Reagan signed into law the Tax Reform Act of 1986, he boasted, "Millions of the working poor will be dropped from the tax rolls altogether, and families will get a long-overdue break with lower rates and an almost doubled personal exemption."

Both the initial Reagan tax cuts of 1981 and indexing income taxes to inflation in 1985 also freed the middle and working classes from much of their federal tax burden.

In the 1990s, the Republican-controlled Gingrich Congress passed a $500-per-child tax credit that also wiped out the income tax liability of many low- to moderate-income households. George W. Bush expanded the child tax credit and also signed tax cuts that reduced the bottom marginal income tax rate from 15 percent to 10 percent. Both moves increased the percentage of people not paying income tax.

Far from enabling the growth of government, tax relief for the working poor and middle class has made it possible to enact across-the-board tax cuts that apply even to upper-income earners. Ramesh Ponnuru writes in *National Review*, "Conservatives cannot really believe that it was a flaw in America's founding that nobody paid income taxes to the federal government for almost all of the country's history before the welfare state."

Even some beneficiaries of the welfare state voted against the party of big government. Romney carried senior citizens on Social Security and Medicare, as did John McCain in 2008, and by a wider margin that Bush did in 2004 despite a drop in support for the Republican presidential ticket overall. An increase in food stamps and unemployment didn't prevent the GOP from winning the 2010 midterm elections.

But it's nevertheless a concern shared by many conservatives. John Hinderaker of the popular blog Power Line is one example: "With over 100 million Americans receiving federal welfare benefits, millions more going on Social Security disability, and many millions on top of that living on entitlement programs—not to mention enormous numbers of public employees—we may have gotten to the point where the government economy is more important, in the short term, than the real economy."

People who draw benefits from a particular government program don't like to see cuts, even if they take a dim view of big government in general. They may also vote for candidates or political parties seen as protective of those benefits.

The purpose of a limited-government political movement shouldn't be to maximize the number of people paying taxes, even when that means subjecting people on subsistence levels of income to taxation. Romney was also wrong to speak as if policies that promote economic growth, lower taxes, and unshackle the free market don't ultimately benefit everyone, rather than just the select few.

Nevertheless, we shouldn't be naïve about the effects of government dependency on voting patterns. Even if the "makers-versus-takers" narrative hasn't been the decisive factor in recent elections, big government by its very nature creates its own constituency—even when its clients and dependents know that high taxes and spending are generally harmful. Some of the same people telling pollsters they would like a smaller government or that Washington is a threat will vote to preserve entitlement spending that is flowing their way.

Some of the fastest-growing demographic groups in the United States are assimilating into the welfare state, a development that limited the Republicans' electoral appeal in 2012. Hispanic Americans, for instance, have a high rate of participation in the labor force but are still disproportionately poor. Many Latino households therefore rely on means-tested government programs for some part of their income.

Romney's dismissal of Hispanic voters as the recipient of "gifts" was certainly damaging, but an analysis of Census Bureau data by the researcher Steve Camarota finds that one in five Hispanic citizens lives in poverty; that one in four Hispanic men between the ages of twenty-five and fifty-five is out of work; that half of all Hispanic households with children are headed by single mothers, and that 55 percent use some form of welfare.

Taking a look at the unmarried women who head half of Hispanic American households, the conservative columnist Pat Buchanan asks, "Why should this woman vote for a party that will cut taxes she does not pay, but reduce benefits she does receive?"[17]

It's a question that Republicans are going to have to answer if they want to improve upon Romney's 27 percent of the Hispanic vote in coming elections. And it is a question that anyone who wants a smaller federal government will have to answer. Right now that group does not include most Hispanic Americans. According to a *Washington Post* poll, 67 percent of Hispanics prefer a larger government that provides more services. This prompted the *Post*'s reporter Aaron Blake to observe, "Latinos are very much in line with the Democratic Party when it comes to how much government should do."[18]

Maybe by speaking the language of growth, opportunity, and upward mobility—and ditching the inelegant Romneyesque language of disdain—Republicans can persuade Hispanics to "vote their aspirations rather than their circumstances," as one advocate of GOP Latino outreach advised.

"These are people who are coming here because of our system of liberties and opportunities. They come here, they're very entrepreneurial, they're opening businesses three times as fast as the country as a whole," Alfonso Aguilar of the Latino Partnership for Conservative Principles told the *Washington Times*.[19] Perhaps reminding them of the big governments they chose to leave behind, which few of them would characterize as successful in promoting prosperity, may also help.

But the bottom line is that even in a political culture as skeptical of government as ours, big government has a lot of supporters. It is easier to oppose federal spending in the abstract than to advocate cuts to specific programs with tangible benefits. To use the language of political science and economics, government comes with concentrated benefits and diffuse costs.

Everyone sees the "shovel-ready projects" promoted by the Obama stimulus package. (Well, as it turns out, not many people saw them because it took the government so long to get its act together—as Obama himself quipped, "Shovel-ready was not as shovel-ready as we expected." But the idea in principle still stands.) Not as many people see the jobs that were never created or the projects that didn't get off the ground because resources were misallocated by politicians or bureaucrats.

THE MISSING LIBERTARIANS

There have always been some people who want a drastically smaller federal government and who vote for different candidates than do most other Americans who prefer smaller government. But these voters are deserting Republican candidates in large enough numbers and in close enough elections for people to notice.

Outlets as diverse as *Human Events* and the left-wing blog Daily Kos have asked if Libertarian candidates might have cost the GOP as many as nine races in 2012. That's the number of contests in which the Libertarian candidate received more votes than the Democrat's margin of victory over the Republican candidate.

"What's more, none of these involved the typical 1 or maybe 2 percent you ordinarily expect a Lib[ertarian] to garner," wrote the Daily Kos's David Nir. "Looking at the three-way vote, all but one were over 3 percent, and three took 6 percent or more, with a high of 6.5 percent in the Montana Senate race. These definitely seem like unusually high figures."

Also unusually high were the Libertarian presidential candidate's vote totals. Gary Johnson, a former two-term Republican governor of New Mexico who briefly sought the GOP presidential nomination, received more than 1.2 million votes. That is the highest popular vote received by any Libertarian presidential nominee in the party's more than forty-year history and its second-highest percentage of the national vote.

Remember, according to the exit polls, Obama received a higher percentage of the big-government vote than Romney did of the small-government vote. Obama had done more to *deserve* the big-government vote than Romney did the small-government vote. Might not Johnson's showing also have been a factor?

Let's go back to the down-ballot races. In Montana, the incumbent Democratic senator, Jon Tester, beat the Republican Denny Rehberg by 18,764 votes. But the Libertarian Dan Cox drew 31,287 votes for 6.5 percent of the total—a high for a Libertarian statewide candidate and more than enough to effect the outcome.

Then there was the Senate race in Indiana, where Democratic congressman Joe Donnelly won by a margin of 131,575 votes over State Treasurer Richard Mourdock, who made headlines earlier in the year by defeating six-term senator Richard Lugar in the GOP primary. Mourdock made headlines again when he appeared to say that rape was part of God's plan while answering an abortion-related question during a debate.

The Libertarian nominee, Andrew Horning, was included in the debates with Donnelly and Mourdock. (His answers didn't make national headlines, for good or for ill.) Horning won 146,453 votes, or 5.8 percent of the total. That was, again, more than Donnelly's winning margin, in a race where many voters favoring small government might have been looking for an alternative to the Republican candidate.

In fairness, we can't assume that every vote cast for a Libertarian candidate would have otherwise gone to a Republican. Some might have preferred Democrats on foreign policy, civil liberties, or social issues. Others will vote Libertarian Party no matter what. A person who will vote Libertarian against Ron Paul Republicans like Kerry Bentovolio or Justin Amash is not someone whose vote the GOP is likely to win in the foreseeable future.

For that reason, Republicans would have lost most of the nine races highlighted by Daily Kos even if the Libertarian Party did not exist. But would it have lost *all* of them, including the Montana and Indiana Senate races?

A typical Libertarian presidential candidate receives between 300,000 and 400,000 votes, so something in that range could be said to be the party's baseline presidential vote. Bob Barr, a former Republican congressman, received over 523,000 votes as the Libertarian nominee in 2008. That means Johnson won over 730,000 more votes than Barr, who was on the high end of the Libertarian presidential vote range and did more than most to appeal to disgruntled Republican voters. (The 1980 Libertarian ticket of Ed Clark and David Koch, by contrast, sold their platform as "low-tax liberalism.") It strains credulity to think none of Johnson's above-average vote was available to Republicans.

Unlike Cox or Horning, Johnson didn't win enough votes to change the outcome of the presidential election, even if Romney had taken 100 percent of his support. But one post-election analysis did note that Obama's margin of victory in four key battleground states that could have turned the election—New Hampshire, Florida, Ohio, and Virginia—was less than Ron Paul's 2012 primary vote totals.[20] How many of those Paul voters ended up pulling the lever for Romney rather than voting for a third-party candidate, writing in Paul, or staying home? Nobody knows. But these figures add to the anecdotal, if not scientific, evidence that the GOP missed out on an appreciable part of the liberty vote.

Republican senator John Thune of South Dakota lost his first Senate race back in 2002 by a mere 524 votes. In that contest, the Libertarian, Kurt Evans, pulled more than 31,000 votes. Longtime *Human Events* political reporter John Gizzi asked Thune if he felt Evans was a "spoiler" in that race:

> "No doubt about it," Thune shot back without hesitation. "He ran to the right of me. I remember when (Evans) came in to tell me he was going to run and I said, 'You know Kurt, it's going to be a really close race. You could be the difference in this.' And he said, 'I've been called by God to do this,' and I said, 'I understand. I can't tell you not to do this. I'm just telling you as a practical matter that in a really close race in this state, that whatever you

take away is coming out of our vote total.' But he went ahead and did it anyway, so you're right."[21]

Even if it could be established beyond a shadow of a doubt that Libertarians cost the GOP elections, it doesn't follow that Republicans are entitled to these votes. In the Montana Senate race, for example, Rehberg said he would vote against Paul Ryan's Medicare reforms because they cut spending too much, and he was arguably worse on civil liberties than his Democratic opponent.

Romney's failings from a small-government perspective are many, and I'll discuss them later. Suffice it to say that a major problem for those who want less government is that most voters are not systematical small-government political thinkers—and those who are remain divided in critical races.

CHAPTER THREE

THE SECOND BIG-GOVERNMENT PARTY

Before Ron Paul retired from Congress, his Washington colleagues gathered to honor him one last time. In twelve terms as a Republican congressman from Texas, Paul never voted for a tax increase, debt ceiling extension, or unbalanced budget.

Originally an obstetrician-gynecologist—he delivered four thousand babies, and he owed some of his political success to their families' votes—he was nicknamed "Dr. No" for his record of opposing all legislation not expressly authorized by the Constitution. After decades of saying no to unconstitutional bills, Paul was now saying good-bye.

Good-bye to the nation's capital, at least. Paul's two Republican presidential campaigns had done more to spread his message than his many years in the House. He was a rare conservative political figure whose appeal to younger voters could rival Obama's. His son Rand was now representing Kentucky in the Senate. A young disciple named Justin Amash held Gerald Ford's old seat in the Michigan House delegation.

You don't need to agree with Ron Paul on every issue—I don't—to recognize that his political courage was uncommon. Most members of Congress would never be as consistent in their opposition to big government, even if they wanted to be.

A diverse crowd was on hand to pay tribute to Paul at his retirement dinner in the Library of Congress. Longtime liberal Democratic congressman Dennis Kucinich, who wanted to create a federal Department of Peace to complement the Department of Defense, rubbed elbows with Senate Republican leader Mitch McConnell. Senator Jim DeMint, the conservative kingmaker from South Carolina, gave an early speech before the meals were served.

There were many other heartfelt tributes before the night was over. But perhaps the most moving came from Roscoe Bartlett, a Republican congressman from Maryland and a strong conservative. He first offered some tender recollections about his retiring colleague. But what he had to say about his own service in the House was just as poignant—and revealing. "I haven't always voted with Ron Paul," Bartlett admitted. "Not because I disagreed with him, necessarily, but because I didn't think I could and then come back here."[1]

Bartlett was a staunch conservative, first elected in 1992 at the age of sixty-six. Having already taught anatomy, physiology, and zoology at the college level, Bartlett pursued political office as something of a retirement gig. He was a true believer who wanted to make a difference, and his voting record was more principled than average. Indeed, any list of standout congressional conservatives of the last twenty years would be woefully incomplete without Bartlett's name.

Nevertheless, he acknowledged that even he sometimes did not vote his conscience on big issues—war and peace, the national debt, our political inheritance from the Founding Fathers—out of fear of the political consequences. If Roscoe Bartlett couldn't buck the tide and cast difficult votes, who could? And what hope is there for the Republican Party?

A few weeks after Ron Paul's retirement dinner, Bartlett was defeated in his bid for reelection. He was out of Congress at the age of eighty-six. Worrying about losing occasionally kept him from casting votes he believed were right, yet he ultimately lost anyway—a victim of hostile redistricting.

The point isn't to criticize Bartlett as much as to say there is a moral to this story for the Republican Party. One of the biggest obstacles to defeating limited government is the absence of a real limited-government party. The GOP is supposed to stand for freedom, fiscal responsibility, and constitutionally limited government. At crucial times, it has done anything but that.

THE PARADOX OF PAUL RYAN

Let's consider the career of a Republican congressman more prominent than Bartlett, one who has in the last few years emerged as a major leader in the party. No single figure represents the conflict between the aspirations and the reality of the modern GOP better than Paul Ryan.

Before Ryan became Mitt Romney's running mate, he was a devoted conservative policy wonk. Ryan worked for Empower America, a think tank founded by Jack Kemp and Bill Bennett, two advocates of an entrepreneurial and innovative post-Reagan conservatism.

Kemp had served nine terms in the House, where he crafted the legislation that inspired Reagan's supply-side revolution, before becoming secretary of housing and urban development under

George H. W. Bush. Bennett was Reagan's most prominent education secretary. Empower America was originally seen as the incuba-
tor of ideas that would serve a Kemp or Bennett presidency.

Kemp briefly sought the Republican nomination in 1988, when
he had little chance of securing it. Bennett never did, despite a "draft
Bill" movement by some social conservatives in 1996. But Empower
America continued to generate ideas and policy proposals based on
free markets—school choice, tax incentives for small businessmen
from the suburbs to the inner city, deregulation, and pro-growth tax
policy.

That's where Ryan cut his teeth. He was elected to Congress from
Wisconsin in 1998 at the age of twenty-eight. That's the same year
the state reelected Russ Feingold, one of the most liberal Democrats
in the Senate. Ryan often reminds audiences that he didn't come
from a safe Republican district. His constituents went for Michael
Dukakis in 1988, Bill Clinton in 1992 and 1996, Al Gore in 2000, and
Barack Obama in 2008.

"We beat John Kerry, by the way, because nobody can relate to
that guy," Ryan often quips about his district's 2004 vote for George
W. Bush. "You come to Wisconsin and talk about *Lambert* Field
instead of Lambeau and there's no way you're going to win in our
area."[2]

During his time in Congress, Ryan has stood—frequently almost
alone—against the status quo of both parties on spending. The
unfunded liabilities of Social Security and Medicare, entitlement
programs designed for a country with very different demographics,
are the biggest drivers of the long-term debt. The specifics of Ryan's
proposals have varied over the years, but the basic framework of his
reforms has been consistent: convert Medicare from a government-
run, single-payer system to the premium-support model (part of a
larger strategy of reducing health care costs through consumer
choice and market competition); turn programs like Medicaid over

to the states with block grants, and cap their growth; and cut non-defense discretionary spending as much as is practicable and politically achievable.

When Ryan unveiled his plan as the "Roadmap for America's Future," it might as well have been a map to the lost city of Atlantis. Members of the House Republican leadership wanted nothing to do with it. Colleagues offered tepid praise, calling it essentially a discussion-starter—a discussion it was clear few of them hoped to have.

The Roadmap received this frosty response in spite of Ryan's effort to make his proposals politically saleable as well as arithmetically sound. The Medicare premium-support model was based partly on ideas borrowed from centrist Democrats like former Clinton budget adviser Alice Rivlin. Senator Ron Wyden, a liberal Democrat from Oregon, supported other versions of the proposal. The Medicare reforms were gradual, affecting no current retirees or benefits. The original Roadmap didn't even balance the budget until 2063.

But Ryan persevered. His willingness to take on these tough issues won him the respect of his colleagues. He gradually worked his way up the ranks and became the top Republican on the House Budget Committee, leapfrogging more senior members. After the GOP won control of the House in the 2010 midterm elections, Ryan became chairman.

The Roadmap was refined and renamed "The Path to Prosperity." The plan's purpose was threefold: (1) make Medicare and eventually the other big entitlements solvent over the long term, (2) reduce the debt-to-GDP ratio to a sustainable level, and (3) limit the federal tax burden to something approximating its post-World War II norm as a percentage of the economy.

With Ryan now chairman of the Budget Committee, the Path to Prosperity wasn't just another conservative think tank white paper.

It was the official budget proposal of Republicans in the House. The Ryan budget was now the GOP's budget, for better or worse.

By the end of 2012, Ryan's budget had twice passed the full House, where Obama's fiscal 2012 budget was rejected by a vote of 414 to 0. None of Obama's budgets has won a single vote from a member of either house of Congress. That's not the only way Ryan's budget compares favorably with Obama's: it reduces spending by $3 trillion, cuts deficits by $5 trillion, and averts $2 trillion in tax increases that would otherwise occur if the president's budget blueprints became law. Ryan would repeal Obamacare and transform—critics say "voucher out"—Medicare.

Since Reagan, Republicans have been the party of tax cuts. They have sought to limit federal revenues to roughly one-fifth of GDP or less. Ryan finally put the congressional wing of the party on record in favor of reining in spending enough to make that tax burden sustainable. Until Ryan, the parties' *modus vivendi* gave Republicans their tax rates and Democrats their spending programs at the cost of perpetual deficit spending.

But deficits, especially in the range of a trillion dollars per year, cannot go on forever. "If something cannot go on forever," James Burnham once observed, "it will stop." Obama responded to the deficits by trying to raise taxes. The Ryan Republicans called for bringing spending in line with taxes.

ROADMAP TO BIG GOVERNMENT

Ryan's victories constituted a major breakthrough in Republican thinking on the budget, but there was another side of the Wisconsin congressman: during the period when many Republicans say they "lost [their] way," Ryan was leading the way for bigger government.

Ryan voted for No Child Left Behind, growing the size of a federal Department of Education that Republicans had pledged to abolish as recently as 1996. He not only supported the 2003 Medicare prescription drug benefit bill, but he exhorted other members to do the same. Ryan was thus instrumental in the creation of the biggest new entitlement since Lyndon Johnson was president, one that added upwards of $20 trillion to Medicare's unfunded liabilities.

Medicare Part D, as we shall see, was no minor deviation from the principle of limited government. "The GOP, for all intents and purposes, had become the party of Big Government," wrote Stephen Slivinski, an expert on tax and budget policy who tells this sad story in his book *Buck Wild*. "Every spending binge before this was just practice. The Medicare drug vote was the coming-out party."[3]

Then came the $700 billion Wall Street bailout known as the Troubled Asset Relief Program. At first, House Republicans helped defeat TARP, but George W. Bush, Barack Obama, and John McCain decided to take another swing. Ryan stood with them, pleading with GOP colleagues to vote for TARP. In fact, he was one of only twenty Republicans to do so.

"I believe we were on the cusp of a deflationary spiral which would have created a depression," Ryan explained to the *Daily Caller*. "If we would have allowed that to happen, I think we would have had a big government agenda sweeping through this country so fast that we wouldn't have recovered from it."[4] Like Obama, Ryan argued that TARP rescued America from even worse economic depths. Like Bush, he contended that we had to abandon the free market in order to save it.

Ryan, hailing from a union-heavy state with car manufacturing jobs, also voted for the auto bailout. He told the *New York Times*, "I'm not trying to win an award from the Cato Institute."[5]

Some conservatives have even complained about Ryan's work to make his budgets more saleable to other Republicans. The Club for Growth, one of the most influential fiscal watchdog groups on the right, pointed out that the most recent version of Ryan's budget plan didn't balance the budget until 2040. It also denounced House Republicans for failing to implement all the spending cuts mandated by the failure of the "super committee," the bipartisan legislative task force that attempted to come up with savings in order to offset the increase in the debt ceiling in 2011. The organization's president, Chris Chocola, himself a former Republican congressman, said, "The Club for Growth urges Republicans to support a budget that balances in the near future and complies with the Budget Control Act" (the legislation that resolved the 2011 debt-ceiling impasse).[6]

A blogger affiliated with FreedomWorks complained, "Unfortunately, [Ryan's] plan doesn't really try to balance the budget or specify a single cabinet agency for elimination." The blogger also criticized Ryan for leaving defense and Social Security, two of the biggest line items in the federal budget, off the table.

Two conservative rising stars among the House freshmen, Representatives Tim Huelskamp of Kansas and Justin Amash of Michigan, broke party lines in voting against the Ryan budget in committee. As a result, the Budget Committee approved it by only a narrow nineteen-to-eighteen vote. The margin in the full House was much wider, with Republican opposition rising only slightly from four "no" votes in 2011 to ten the following year.

The journalist Peter Suderman explained the paradox of Paul Ryan. "For advocates of limited government, Ryan remains one of the most important allies in Congress," he wrote during the days of the early Roadmap. "But those advocates can't help but notice that the best hope for fiscal responsibility and free market reform is a plan to balance the budget 50 years from now that will never, ever pass."[7]

Ryan is the man who came up with the budget plan to give the Tea Party achievable goals while making it an intellectually coherent movement. He also cast many of the votes that gave rise to the Tea Party in the first place, with a record on those issues that got lesser Republicans defeated in primaries.

TEAM PLAYERS

During the 2012 Republican primaries, the leading conservative alternative to Mitt Romney was Rick Santorum, a former senator from Pennsylvania. Santorum won his first statewide race as part of the GOP's 1994 tidal wave. His record had much to recommend it. He championed the ill-fated Medicare reforms of 1995, which would have helped the program's solvency and saved taxpayers money. Santorum was a key figure in the fight for welfare reform. He was also a pro-life stalwart.

When George W. Bush replaced Bill Clinton as president, a funny thing happened to Santorum's voting record. He supported No Child Left Behind. He voted for the unfunded Medicare prescription drug benefit. He voted for the pork-laden 2005 highway bill that included the earmark for the "Bridge to Nowhere." Santorum had voted against such a bill just the year before. After it passed anyway, he was quoted as joking, "Never get between a congressman and asphalt because you will get run over."[8]

Why did Santorum run over his own record of supporting limited government? In a February 2012 Republican candidates' debate in which he was pressed on his vote for No Child Left Behind, he offered a surprisingly frank assessment. "When you're part of the team, sometimes you take one for the team for the leader, and I made a mistake," Santorum said. "You know, politics is a team sport, folks. Sometimes you've got to rally together and do something."[9]

Do something? Like the opposite of what you came to Washington to do—namely, shrink government and restore the Constitution?

The remark was widely and justifiably panned. Even Romney had the audacity to pile on Santorum. "I wonder which team he was taking it for," he told the Associated Builders and Contractors. "My team is the American people, not the insiders in Washington."[10]

Romney went so far as to say, "I've never seen a politician explain in so many ways why he voted against his principles."

It's tempting to ask him to look in the mirror, but there were plenty of places within the Republican Party to look for selective opposition to big government. In fact, you needed look no further than Santorum's main competitor for the conservative vote, Newt Gingrich.

As the House speaker of the original '94 "revolution" majority, Gingrich was in a real sense the hero of the last war. But once he wielded the gavel, he did a lot to undermine the government-cutters in the Republican caucus behind the scenes. After he was forced out of the speakership in 1998, Gingrich advocated big government in full public view.

Gingrich tried to rally Republicans behind the Medicare prescription drug benefit. "Every conservative member of Congress should vote for this Medicare bill," he wrote. "It is the most important reorganization of our nation's healthcare system since the original Medicare Bill of 1965 and the largest and most positive change in direction for the health system in 60 years for people over 65."

Newt undoubtedly thought he was being a team player.

On the individual mandate to purchase health insurance, Gingrich's record was as bad as Obama's or Romney's. That record led to this fascinating exchange between Romney and Gingrich at a Republican presidential debate in Las Vegas:

> *Gingrich*: So there's a lot of big government behind Romneycare. Not as much as Obamacare, but a heck of a lot more than your campaign is admitting.
>
> *Romney*: Actually, Newt, we got the idea of an individual mandate from you.
>
> *Gingrich*: That's not true. You got it from the Heritage Foundation.
>
> *Romney*: Yes, we got it from you, and you got it from the Heritage Foundation and from you [sic].
>
> *Gingrich*: Wait a second. What you just said is not true. You did not get that from me. You got it from the Heritage Foundation.
>
> *Romney*: And you never supported them?
>
> *Gingrich*: I agree with them, but I'm just saying, what you said to this audience just now plain wasn't true.
>
> *Romney*: OK. Let me ask, have you supported in the past an individual mandate?
>
> *Gingrich*: I absolutely did, with the Heritage Foundation against Hillarycare.[11]

So there you had two leading candidates to replace Obama, in an election fought in part on the issue of repealing and replacing Obamacare, highlighting their past support for the individual mandate and arguing over who thought of it first—all while repeatedly implicating the nation's most influential conservative think tank.

In her opening statement at that debate, Michele Bachmann quipped, "And this is one night when I hope what happens in Vegas doesn't stay in Vegas." After that Romney-Gingrich spat, most conservatives and Republicans probably hoped otherwise.

The point here isn't to jump on any particular candidate. Even Ron Paul—in many respects the gold standard (naturally) of constitutional conservatism—had to explain why he pushed earmarks requesting funding for purely local projects in his district. Although he ultimately voted against the appropriations bills, the earmarks at least obscured his message. "I love Ron Paul!" Tom DeLay once told me during an interview. "Who do you think got him all his earmarks?"

Everybody should be judged on his full record. But giving putatively small-government politicians too many excuses for growing government has predictably led to bigger and bigger government.

LYNDON B. BUSH

When Barack Obama is challenged on his trillion-dollar deficits, he has a convenient excuse: blame George W. Bush.

Obama says everything was just fine with the Clinton budget surpluses until "the money was spent on trillions of dollars in new tax cuts, while two wars and an expensive prescription drug program were simply added to our nation's credit card."

He repeated a variant of this line during the presidential debates: "And we know where [the deficit] came from: two wars that were paid for on a credit card; two tax cuts that were not paid for; and a whole bunch of programs that were not paid for; and then a massive economic crisis."[12]

Joe Biden even blamed Bush-era spending for the recession in his 2012 debate with Paul Ryan: "And, by the way, they talk about this Great Recession as if it fell out of the sky, like, 'Oh, my goodness, where did it come from?' It came from this man voting to put two wars on a credit card, to at the same time put a prescription drug benefit on the credit card, a trillion-dollar tax cut for the very wealthy."[13]

In his typical fashion, the vice president pressed on without regard for the facts: "I was there. I voted against them. I said, no, we can't afford that." Biden actually voted for the two unfunded wars and an even bigger version of the prescription drug benefit, which he didn't plan to fund either. He did vote against the tax cuts, however.

Obama can't be held responsible for voting for the wars, since he wasn't in the Senate yet. (He said in speeches at the time that he supported the invasion of Afghanistan after the 9/11 terrorist attacks but not the invasion of Iraq.) But as president, Obama continued the Iraq war until the Iraqis kicked us out—the final troops were withdrawn when no status-of-forces agreement could be reached— without trying to pay for it. He escalated the war in Afghanistan without trying to pay for it. He extended the Bush tax cuts in 2010 without trying to pay for them. He did not try to repeal or pay for the "expensive" prescription drug benefit or other programs. Obama didn't take any responsibility for the role his own policies played in enlarging the deficits either. In this telling, there were no increases in discretionary spending, no stimulus, and the national debt did not rise faster in three years and two months under him ($4.939 trillion) than it did in eight years under Bush ($4.899 trillion).

But Obama does have a point about spending under his predecessor. In exit polls in the 2012 election, about half the voters still blamed Bush for the nation's economic woes, the figure most likely to have doomed Romney's election prospects. Worse, Bush's big spending clearly set the stage for Obama's while irreparably harming Republican fiscal credibility—not least by making big-spending "team players" out of Ryan, Santorum, and a generation of promising Republican leaders.

Under Bush, the national debt skyrocketed from $5.7 trillion to $10.7 trillion. A $128 billion surplus was gradually turned into a nearly $455 billion deficit—on the way to $1.2 trillion. As the Heritage Foundation's Brian Riedl has pointed out, Congressional Budget Office data show that the tax cuts caused at most 14 percent of this swing, assuming no pro-growth effects. Tax cuts on those making more than $250,000 per year accounted for just 4 percent.

During Bush's first six years in office, inflation-adjusted discretionary spending—the portion of the federal budget set annually by the president and Congress—increased faster than when Lyndon Johnson was president. From 1963 to 1969, discretionary spending adjusted for inflation increased by 4.6 percent annually. From 2001 to 2007, it increased 5.3 percent a year. Without adjusting for inflation, discretionary spending went up 48.5 percent in Bush's first term alone. That's more than twice as fast as it rose in Clinton's two terms. This trend held up over the course of Bush's entire presidency. After eight years of Clinton, spending went up just 11 percent. At the conclusion of Bush's two terms, it was up 104 percent.

Bush shouldn't be let off the hook for entitlement spending, either—not with his deficit-financed Medicare Part D. And like LBJ, Bush spent money on guns and butter at the same time. Most postwar presidents paid for increases in the defense budget with lower nondefense spending or financed social programs with smaller (or at least slower-growing) defense budgets.

"Only two Cold War presidents after 1964, Johnson and Carter, presided over real increases in both the defense and nondefense budget," observes Stephen Slivinski. "George W. Bush's tenure, however, is a return to the Johnson and Carter philosophy of budgeting: across-the-board increases in everything."[14]

The right rallied behind Bush despite all the spending because of the war on terror following the 9/11 attacks, but the fight against terrorism itself wasn't the main reason for government's growth. A Cato Institute study concluded that even after excluding all homeland security-related spending—some of which certainly should be included—Bush was still the biggest-spending president in thirty years.

After federal spending declined to 18.4 percent of GDP under Clinton and the 1990s Republican-controlled Congress, it climbed back to 20.51 percent per year on average under Bush. Federal expenditures were growing 6 to 7 percent per annum, compared with about 11 percent under Obama and the Democratic Congress.

"A $220 billion increase isn't nothing, and the damage it will do is likely to be compounded by the fact that it represents an addition to the baseline," writes *National Review*'s Stephen Spruiell of the difference between Obama and Bush's spending. "But it isn't a gargantuan blowout compared to where we would be if the Bush-Reid-Pelosi trends had continued."[15]

The Wall Street bailouts, the auto bailouts, and even the first attempts at stimulus all date back to Bush. The main reason no one could get a clear shot at Obama's big-government record is that Bush sowed the seeds for it.

BIG-GOVERNMENT CONSERVATISM

Much of this Bush-era government growth was by design. The idea was that No Child Left Behind would negate the traditional Democratic advantage on education issues; the prescription drug benefit would similarly take Medicare away from the Democrats. Soccer moms, seniors, and Hispanics would become part of the "permanent Republican majority." It worked only if you define "permanent" as five years. And even then, the war on terror and social issues played a large role in Republican political successes.

Former Bush speechwriter Michael Gerson later recalled in the *Washington Post*:

> In his 2006 State of the Union address, which I helped write, President George W. Bush proposed a 22-percent increase in clean-energy research at the Energy Department, a doubling of basic research in the physical sciences and the training of 70,000 high school teachers to instruct Advanced Placement courses in math and science. I have no idea if these "investments" passed or made much difference. I doubt anyone knows.[16]

Even Bush's free-market ideas, such as the "ownership society," relied heavily on activist government. Consider Fred Barnes's explanation of "big government conservatism" in the *Wall Street Journal*. "They simply believe in using what would normally be seen as liberal means—activist government—for conservative ends," he writes. "And they're willing to spend more and increase the size of government in the process."[17] That means accepting or even expanding the social-welfare programs that Democrats built while channeling the dollars toward faith-based initiatives, abstinence-only sex education, marriage-promotion schemes, and other projects amenable to GOP constituencies. "The essence of Bush's big government conservatism is a trade-off," Barnes continues. "To gain free-market reforms and expand individual choice, he's willing to broaden programs and increase spending."

The authors of *Grand New Party*, Ross Douthat and Reihan Salam, make a similar point: "Rather than target the 'supply-side' of government, or the amount of government spending, Bush's focus was on the 'demand-side,' or the need for government services."[18]

But in every case, free-market reforms and individual choice gave way to big government. Most of the meaningful school choice provisions were stripped from No Child Left Behind before the bill passed Congress. And even with Medicare Advantage—a free-market health savings account component of the prescription drug benefit—Medicare Part D still increased Medicare spending and unfunded liabilities.

Not coincidentally, Medicare Advantage was the first thing Obama and his Democratic majorities targeted for elimination. In its place, they wanted to impose price controls on prescriptions through the Bush drug benefit. They failed, but it is an example of how this approach can yield even bigger government.

In 2006, before the recession hit, enrollment in twenty-five major federal programs—from Medicaid to Pell Grants—had increased 17 percent since 2000, while the population increased by just 5 percent over the same period. The economy played a role, but so did the demand-side logic of big-government conservatism: to help encourage work over welfare, Congress expanded eligibility for some other public aid programs. Allowing low-income workers who own cars worth more than $4,650 to qualify for food stamps extended the benefit to an estimated 2.7 million people, buying more "independence" from one program with greater dependence on another. Big-government conservatism thus failed on its own terms.

NOT JUST BUSH

But it would be a mistake to blame all Republican fiscal irresponsibility on Bush. The truth is that the GOP Congress's commitment to fiscal discipline collapsed around 1998, before Bush even declared his candidacy. That was the year the GOP congressional majority first proposed outspending Bill Clinton.

Even before Bush said, "[W]hen somebody hurts, government has got to move," Republican senator Dan Coats of Indiana and GOP House Budget Committee chairman John Kasich wrote in the *Washington Times*, "The fact that government programs have not worked is no excuse for those in government not to act."

More than a decade after the '94 revolution, a Cato analysis found that the combined inflation-adjusted budgets of the 101 largest programs the GOP had pledged to eliminate had in fact grown by 27 percent. Republicans had controlled the House for that entire time and held the Senate for most of that period.

In Bush's first term, the GOP Congress passed budgets that spent $91 billion more than the president requested. Many Republicans denied that there was even a problem. Declaring "ongoing victory" in the war against runaway federal spending, House Majority Leader Tom DeLay boasted, "[A]fter eleven years of Republican majority we've pared it down pretty good." He said this while fiscal conservatives were clamoring for him not to add to the $331 billion deficit—which had only recently been a surplus—in the aftermath of Hurricane Katrina. "My answer to those that want to offset the spending is sure, bring me the offsets, I'll be glad to do it," DeLay continued. "But nobody has been able to come up with any yet."[19]

The problem, then as now, is not that there's no spending to cut. It's that there are always a trillion reasons not to cut it.

CHAPTER FOUR

BIG GOVERNMENT'S PUBLICISTS

I f you believe the self-congratulatory mythology that surrounds the mainstream media, reporters are inherently skeptical of those in power. A journalist's proper relationship with government, legend has it, is adversarial. Think of Watergate, the Pentagon Papers, *The Selling of the President 1968*.

Notice how all the really good examples date back to the Nixon years? The civil libertarian blogger Glenn Greenwald, a liberal, quipped, "The smartest thing Dan Ellsberg ever did was get persecuted by a GOP President rather than a Democrat, or else he'd have had little support."

"Journalists didn't wake up one morning and decide to be cynical," wrote Rem Rieder, editor of the *American Journalism Review*. "What happened is that politics has become a highly manipulative affair, dominated by consultants and spin doctors and deceptive television ads and constantly shifting positions."[1]

That's a reasonably accurate portrayal of American politics, but it's an incomplete picture of the journalists who cover it. The *New York Times* admitted in the summer of 2012 that the Obama and Romney campaigns frequently demanded veto power over the quotations reporters used in their stories—and that many, if not most, reporters acceded. "Most reporters, desperate to pick the brains of the president's top strategists, grudgingly agree. After the interviews, they review their notes, check their tape recorders and send in the juiciest sound bites for review," the *Times* reported. "The verdict from the campaign—an operation that prides itself on staying consistently on script—is often no, Barack Obama does not approve this message."

The word among Washington political reporters is that Jim Messina, the manager of Obama's 2012 campaign, has a potty mouth. But mere readers wouldn't know it because he goes through his quotations like an old Hays Code censor and deletes the profanity.

Romney's strategist Stuart Stevens, the *New York Times* says, "is fond of disparaging political opponents by quoting authors like Walt Whitman and referring to historical figures like H. R. Haldeman, Richard Nixon's chief of staff." But Stevens didn't consider his witticisms to be among the news that's fit to print.[2]

If pervasive quotation-approval doesn't convince you that there isn't enough distance between the press and the politicians they cover, perhaps tuning into the annual White House Correspondents' Association Dinner will do the trick. The event has become too cozy even for an establishment figure like Tom Brokaw, the former anchorman of NBC's nightly news. "That's another separation between what we're supposed to be doing and what the people expect us to be doing, and I think that the Washington press corps has to look at that," Brokaw said.[3] A good start, but even he seemed to miss the point. The problem isn't reporters rubbing elbows with George Clooney. It's treating the president, and others who live off our tax dollars and possess the power to send our children to war, as if they are fuzzy celebrities like George Clooney.

An even bigger problem is that, while reporters might be skeptical of the motives of individual politicians or willing to follow the money in pursuit of scandals, they usually give big government the benefit of the doubt when not accepting its premises and assumptions uncritically.

PUBLIC ENEMY #1: GROVER

For example, the media have tended to be sympathetic to raising taxes, especially the top marginal rate, while sounding the alarm about anyone who dares object. The liberal commentator Bill Press likened politicians who sign pledges against tax increases to "traitors."[4] On National Public Radio, the *Washington Post* columnist E. J. Dionne compared Obama's resolve on tax hikes to Abraham Lincoln's commitment to abolishing slavery.[5]

Press and Dionne are open purveyors of liberal opinion who do not pretend to be providing entirely objective coverage. Not so Brian Montopoli, the senior political reporter for CBS News. Even though Republicans have been providing detailed economic arguments against tax increases for thirty years, he can cite only fear of right-wing pressure groups—presumably funded by nefarious plutocrats—as the reason for GOP tax hike reluctance. "For a Republican lawmaker, angering the Club for Growth and other anti-tax groups could result in an influx of outside money that could sink your reelection bid," Montopoli wrote about a group that supports fiscally conservative primary challengers against big-government Republicans. "It's no wonder that when CBS News's political director John Dickerson asked a senior House leadership aide what the chances were that a majority of House Republicans would vote for a tax increase, the response was 'pretty close to zero.'"[6]

The most demonized figure in the media's coverage of the tax debate is Grover Norquist, the founder and president of Americans for Tax Reform and the promoter of the famous Taxpayer Protection Pledge. Though he shares a first name with a Muppet in the important government-funded show *Sesame Street*, when it comes to taxes, Norquist is portrayed as harmful to children and other living things. He simply terrorizes Republicans until they toe his line on taxes. "It's... politically smart to cut the knees out from under Grover Norquist," advised Cokie Roberts on ABC's *This Week*. "I mean this guy is, you know, who is he? He's an unelected lobbyist." Someone needs to inform the country that "the emperor has no clothes," she opined. "To say that, I think is very useful."[7] Useful to whom?

"Why are you so concerned about protecting the vast wealth of America's small percentage of increasingly rich people? Why do you care?" CNN's Piers Morgan (apparently a pauper) asked Norquist. "Everyone is laughing at you from afar."[8]

"Is Grover finally over?" asked the headline of a column Frank Bruni wrote for the *New York Times*. Accompanying Bruni's piece was the editorial statement, "Pledges are for purists, who have no place in a democracy."[9] "Is that how the paper feels about regulatory activists like Ralph Nader?" wondered Clay Waters of the Media Research Center.[10]

When the media aren't depicting Norquist as some kind of strange radical for disliking higher taxes, they are lobbying politicians to violate his organization's pledge against tax increases. Charlie Rose did it on CBS, pressing Senator Bob Corker, a Tennessee Republican, to join unnamed others in saying "I'm going to forgo the [tax] pledge because it is outdated and the country's problems are too big." Norah O'Donnell followed up by asking Corker if he was "willing to also raise the capital gains tax rate."[11] CNN's Soledad O'Brien, never bashful about sharing her emotions with her viewers, actually tore up a copy of the hated pledge while badgering Congressman Jason Chaffetz of Utah to violate it.

"PROFILES IN COURAGE"

Conservatives who stick to their principles on taxes and spending get the Grover Norquist treatment. But more favorable treatment is in store for those who surrender. Those who "grow in office" receive what Tom Bethell of the *American Spectator* calls "Strange New Respect." And indeed, Senator Corker has earned Strange New Respect, distancing himself from Norquist's tax pledge. CNN's Jon Avlon gushed that such Republicans are "profiles in courage," borrowing a famous book title from John F. Kennedy. An unabashed Corker agrees, proclaiming to anyone who would listen, "What it takes is political courage." But one of the senator's constituents suggested otherwise in a letter to the *Nashville Tennessean*: "Sen. Corker went on to say that the challenge we face is a test of 'political courage.' Like disavowing the pledge, two weeks after winning the election?"[12]

When Chief Justice John Roberts sided with the Supreme Court's conservative majority in the *Citizens United* decision, which invalidated part of the McCain-Feingold campaign finance reform law on free-speech grounds, he was the subject of unflattering attention, like Jeffrey Toobin's *New Yorker* article, "Money unlimited: How John Roberts orchestrated the Citizens United decision." "In one sense, the story of the Citizens United case goes back more than a hundred years," Toobin wrote. "It begins in the Gilded Age, when the Supreme Court barred most attempts by the government to ameliorate the harsh effects of market forces. In that era, the Court said, for the first time, that corporations, like people, have constitutional rights."[13]

When Roberts cast the saving vote for Obamacare in the summer of 2012, however, the tone changed. "John Roberts upholds Obamacare and rises above partisanship," wrote Howard Kurtz in the *Daily Beast*. "On Obamacare, it would have been an extraordinary step for five justices to undo it, if only by killing the individual insurance mandate that lies at its heart," Kurtz noted. "With Mitt Romney and congressional Republicans having spent two years crusading against the law, Roberts risked looking like a Bush appointee gutting the signature accomplishment of a Democratic president.[14] Instead, he proved himself capable of rising above ideology and following what he believed to be the law." Jeffrey Toobin himself discovered a new side of Roberts, whose ruling in favor of Obamacare was a "singular act of courage."[15]

Before the Obamacare decision was handed down, David Von Drehle wrote in *Time* about the impending ruling, "But if Roberts is indeed the author, the decision will shed light on which values he holds most highly: the Court's image of fair-mindedness, or the purity of his conservative principles."[16] Nowhere in any of this coverage is it suggested that "conservative principles" and the constitutional law may actually be compatible—or that big government could or should lose. After the decision was handed down, Von Drehle praised Roberts in a *Time* cover story as an example of the "virtue of compromise in an era of Occupiers, Tea Partiers and litmus-testing special interests."[17]

The editors of *Esquire* included Roberts among their "Americans of the Year," praising his "nimbleness" and saying he found a way "to save the court's credibility" after *Citizens United*—this time, presumably, by bending the Constitution to the Left's will.[18] Roberts also made the *Atlantic Monthly*'s annual list of "Brave Thinkers" for a "brave and shrewd" Obamacare ruling responsible for "maintaining the Court's legitimacy."[19] The chief justice shared both of these honors with Lena Dunham, the creator and star of the HBO series *Girls*. Dunham didn't save the credibility of the Supreme Court, but she did "take the soft glow off the 'chick flick'"—apparently a similar accomplishment. "Such is the strange new respect a conservative receives for sustaining liberal priorities," the *Wall Street Journal* editorialized about Roberts's rehabilitation in the press. "Our own view is less effusive, and to expiate his ObamaCare legal sins, a fair punishment would be that he hire Ms. Dunham as a clerk."[20]

This kind of coverage is nothing new. During the debate over creating the State Children's Health Insurance Program (SCHIP) in the 1990s, Senator Orrin Hatch of Utah, a Republican, was praised for his willingness to team up with Democrats on the legislation. Hatch "wanted to lavish taxpayer money on vulnerable children," *Time* reported. He was a "maverick since he left his law practice in Pennsylvania." "It's good for children, it will reduce teenage smoking, and it will lower the deficit," Hatch was quoted as saying. "How can a conservative argue with that?"

Enter Trent Lott, the Republican Senate majority leader, as the villain in *Time*'s morality tale. How can a conservative argue with SCHIP? "Easily enough, if you're Lott, who publicly derided the proposal as a 'big-government program' that would never become law on his watch," the story continued. Lott was supposedly steamed that Hatch "devised a bipartisan bill with Kennedy that Republicans will be hard pressed to oppose" rather than "working with his leadership to produce a Republican proposal." Mean Republicans talked about Hatch behind his back: they "whispered contemptuously about what they described as his sanctimonious air."[21]

Only toward the end of this story do we find an acknowledgment that "in Washington there's no such thing as a pure motive." We learn that the "savvy" Hatch's interest in SCHIP might have been related to his presidential ambitions—and he did run for president in 2000, the next election cycle, although he didn't get very far.

HOW THE MEDIA PROTECT BIG GOVERNMENT

It's probably too much to hope that Hatch learned that media adulation can get you only so far with the voters. The senator not only ran behind the likes of Alan Keyes in his quest for the Republican presidential nomination—well behind, in fact—but faced a surprisingly competitive challenge for the GOP senatorial nomination in 2012. Whether or not he still believes his own press clippings, Hatch won a seventh term in the Senate despite the media's celebration of his transgressions.

These would simply be silly political stories if it weren't for two facts: media coverage does shape how millions of Americans perceive important public debates, and it does influence how political leaders actually behave.

A case in point is the federal government shutdown of 1995. The Republicans had won control of both houses of Congress in the 1994 elections. Bill Clinton was president of the United States. They had come to an impasse over spending. Somehow, it became the conventional wisdom that Republican intransigence was shutting down the government.

Technically, however, it was Clinton's decision to shut down the government. He would not accept the budget passed by Congress because of its spending cuts and handling of Medicare premiums. "The Republicans want to diminish the importance of the Federal Government in American Life," the *New York Times* observed in December 1995. "The President does not, and, in some instances, would expand the Government's role."[22]

Some reports got it right. CNN's website told readers about "talks between Gingrich, Dole and President Clinton, who has threatened to veto the bills that would prevent the government shutdown."[23] The network reported that the House and Senate had passed spending bills and an extension of the debt limit.

The Republicans didn't exactly cover themselves in glory throughout this whole process. One of their eleventh-hour bills to avert a government shutdown would have limited death row appeals—an arguably worthwhile measure, but one that was wholly extraneous to the matter at hand. The Speaker of the House, Newt Gingrich, finally gave the Clinton administration and sympathetic reporters the ammunition they needed. At a press breakfast, Gingrich complained that Clinton hadn't taken the opportunity to discuss the budget with him during flights to and from the funeral of the slain Israeli prime minister, Yitkhak Rabin. Gingrich suggested that he had been asked to leave the plane through a rear door. Many news outlets then began covering the whole budget impasse as if it was the product of a social snub.

The press was merciless. The *New York Daily News* ran a front-page cartoon of Gingrich as a chubby baby in diapers, crying and holding a bottle. The cover headline read, "Cry Baby." The summary of the story was, "Newt's tantrum: He closed down the government because Clinton made him sit at back of the plane."

Re-read that: Newt closed down the government.

Gingrich was portrayed as an arrogant, obnoxious brat with a Rosa Parks complex, who, out of personal pique, was interrupting vital functions of the federal government. Fairly or not, this proved to be a turning point in the standoff.

This coverage of Gingrich wasn't unusual. Shortly after the elections that made him Speaker of the House, *Time* portrayed Gingrich on a Christmas season cover as Ebenezer Scrooge. He was even shown breaking poor Tiny Tim's crutch in half. The headline blared, "Uncle Scrooge: 'Tis the season to bash the poor. But is Newt Gingrich's America really that heartless?" Care to bet what the answer was? This Dickensian theme had surfaced the previous month in the *Baltimore Sun*, which reported, "Resurgent Republicans in Congress under Newt Gingrich are breathing new life into an idea whose time most people thought had already come and gone. They want to bring back orphanages and other forms of state-supervised residences to care for the illegitimate children of young women who would be cut from welfare rolls under their proposals."[24] Are there no workhouses?

A friend had observed, wrote William F. Buckley Jr. at the time, that "he had never seen so concentrated a battery of derogation as has been fired in the past several weeks on Newt Gingrich," including Richard Nixon. Though the abuse was utterly devoid of any balance, Gingrich at least arguably brought a good deal of it on himself. During the second government shutdown—this one lasting two weeks, the longest cessation of operations on record—Republicans began to crack. Bob Dole, the Senate majority leader who was also running for president, took to the floor in early 1996 to declare, "Enough is enough!"

Gingrich himself lost his taste for the fight. When seventeen House Republicans, twelve of them conservative freshmen, voted against re-opening the government, the speaker angrily canceled fundraisers in some of their districts. One of them, Indiana's John Hostettler, later told me that this was the beginning of the end of the Republican revolution. The media portrayed Gingrich's refusal to attend a Hostettler fundraiser as a "spat" that "resulted from an issue on which Hostettler voted further to the right than Gingrich."

It's hard to overstate how big a role the media, with an assist from Gingrich, played in resolving the government shutdown unfavorably to Republicans. Clinton's approval ratings initially fell during the shutdown. The *Washington Post*'s Elizabeth Drew wrote in her book about the new Republican Congress, "Clinton had already moved quite a bit toward the Republicans, and was prepared to move further."[25] But Clinton was masterly in playing to the media, particularly in the aftermath of the showdown. During his 1996 State of the Union address, he showcased Richard Dean, a Social Security Administration employee who survived the Oklahoma City bombing and rescued three people during the attack. The president pointed out that Dean had been furloughed during the first government shutdown and forced to work without pay in the second. To underscore the point, Clinton explicitly rebuked his congressional audience: "Never, ever shut down the government again."

A decade later, Bob Walker, a Republican congressman from Pennsylvania who was a close Gingrich ally, insisted to Fox News reporter Major Garrett that the episode had not been a defeat. "Did we lose an election as a result of it? No. Is there anything really bad that happened congressionally because of the fact that we shut down the government?"[26] That's not how most people remember it, however, in part because of the media firestorm at the time and the narrative that has persisted since then. In my conversations with elected Republicans about the party's reluctance to cut spending, the shutdown comes up again and again—even among those who weren't active in politics, much less in Washington, at the time. "We'll never go back," said one congressional aide. "We'll never go there again."

The debacle is surely seared into the minds of the Republicans who remain. Speaker of the House John Boehner chaired the GOP conference back then. He was the only member of the leadership team to lose his position after the 1996 elections and was forced to work his way back up. The government shutdowns of 1995 are probably in the back of his mind as he negotiates budgets with the Obama administration.

A 2011 poll of political insiders by the *National Journal* tells the story. The well-connected magazine talked to "roughly 200 Democratic and Republican campaign consultants, party officials, strategists, lobbyists, and allied interest group leaders." Democrats said they would benefit from a government shutdown by a margin of 56 percent to 29 percent. Republicans said they would pay the price by 65 percent to 19 percent. "The Republicans look awful if there's a government shutdown and they are seen to have caused it," responded one GOP insider. Another observed, "We always think it's a good idea until we do it and get our butt kicked when real people start suffering for it." One Democratic insider, by contrast, was confident that a shutdown would remind the American people of how much government does to improve their lives.

Karl Rove, the close political adviser to George W. Bush, reminded Republicans, "The shutdowns helped improve Clinton's political standing, boosting both his approval rating and perceptions of him as a strong leader." The president's approval ratings rebounded from the mid-40s before the shutdown to 54 percent after the first one ended in 1995. "Clinton's approval rating never again fell below 50 percent for the remainder of his presidency," Rove observed.

The government shutdown wasn't the only media event of the '90s that continues to drive today's politics. The media also tell a story about the health-care debate at the time that helped influence public impressions of Obamacare. Both Hillary Clinton and Barack Obama portrayed their fights on health care as a battle between people and profits, between insurance companies and those seeking insurance coverage despite their poverty or preexisting conditions.

When the famous "Harry and Louise" commercials, sponsored by the Health Insurance Association of America, began to drive down public support for her health-care plan, Hillary struck back. "What you don't get told in the ad is that it is paid for by insurance companies who think their way is the better way," she said in a November 1993 speech. "They like what is happening today." She asked Americans to stand up to the insurance companies and say, "We want our health care system back." The *New York Times* reported that the biggest health insurers—Prudential, Cigna, Aetna, Metropolitan Life, and Travelers—had in fact broken off from the HIAA and formed the Coalition for Managed Competition. "Managed competition" was the theory on which Hillary Clinton's health care plan was based.

The media generally repeat the conventional wisdom, however. On the rare occasions when they noticed insurers supporting Obamacare, they treated it as a contrast with the Clinton years. The *Los Angeles Times*, for instance, recalled that the industry "scuttled President Clinton's healthcare overhaul bid with ads."

"This sort of faulty history is endemic in politicians' and journalists' discussion of Big Business and Big Government," wrote the journalist Tim Carney. "Typically when Big Business lobbies for Big Government, the media don't notice." When they do, it is presented as a "strange bedfellows" story.[27]

The Harry and Louise ads were reprised in 2008 and 2009, this time with the fictional couple supporting health care reform. The

American Hospital Association and the National Federation of
Independent Business helped pay for the original Harry and Louise
ads; the pro-Obamacare versions of 2009 were funded by the pharmaceutical industry.

MEDIA APPROVAL

Hostile media coverage is certainly effective in making Republicans wary of taking bold stands against big government. But what
about the fawning treatment of those who break ranks? Let's go back
to the Supreme Court's decision upholding Obamacare. As if that
ruling weren't a big enough bombshell, CBS News's chief legal and
political correspondent, Jan Crawford, dropped another one: "Chief
Justice John Roberts initially sided with the Supreme Court's four
conservative justices to strike down the heart of President Obama's
health care reform law, the Affordable Care Act, but later changed
his position and formed an alliance with liberals to uphold the bulk
of the law, according to two sources with specific knowledge of the
deliberations." Roberts "then withstood a month-long, desperate
campaign to bring him back to his original position," apparently led
by Justice Anthony Kennedy.

Why did he switch?

"Some of the conservatives, such as Justice Clarence Thomas,
deliberately avoid news articles on the court when issues are pend-
ing (and avoid some publications altogether, such as *The New York
Times*)," Crawford wrote. "They've explained that they don't want to
be influenced by outside opinion or feel pressure from outlets that
are perceived as liberal. But Roberts pays attention to media coverage," she continued. "As chief justice, he is keenly aware of his
leadership role on the court, and he also is sensitive to how the court
is perceived by the public."

According to this theory, Roberts paid special attention to stories—some of them mentioned in this chapter—warning that the Supreme Court's reputation for nonpartisanship would be harmed if Obamacare were struck down. Roberts was also said to be sensitive to charges that he lied in his confirmation hearings when he emphasized his role as an "umpire," a neutral arbiter practicing judicial restraint.

Some of Roberts's friends and colleagues disputed Crawford's account. Surely it is a grave charge to accuse a respected jurist of acting against his own constitutional judgment to garner favorable press coverage or because he feared the reaction of the *New York Times*.

Conservatives have occasionally been known to overestimate the power of both the mainstream media and the Georgetown cocktail-party circuit. Crawford offered no irrefutable proof, and she stopped short of a definitive judgment. Yet she is a reputable journalist with a network of solid sources, and her story is more than plausible.[28] If a man who has been appointed for life to the highest court in the land and who will never have to face the voters might yield to such pressure, what can we expect from elected politicians in tenuous positions?

THE BIG-GOVERNMENT APPEAL

Most reporters aren't consciously pushing a big-government agenda. They try to be fair and are usually looking for ways to get ahead of their competition. In refuting many of the mainstream media's distortions, in fact, I have relied on reporting by the mainstream media—including, even, the *New York Times* and CBS News. But journalists are an insular group, and they tend to share many political views. This is particularly true of the press corps in

Washington and New York, which disproportionately influence media coverage of hot political topics.

Surveys have shown that reporters distrust business and policies they see as benefiting the wealthy. They're often heedless of the collusion between big business and big government, accepting a facile storyline in which government protects the economic interests of ordinary people against the depredations of the rich and powerful. These same reporters, oddly enough, would probably agree that the government is controlled by the rich and powerful. (And what's richer or more powerful than big government?) But they fail to draw the logical conclusion that government actions are frequently less altruistic than they at first appear.

The mainstream media like to think of themselves as being on the side of the little guy. But a preference for the little guy is the last thing that should dull their skepticism of big government.

CHAPTER FIVE

REAGAN'S LAW

Size doesn't matter. That's what some people say when it comes to government, at least. Ronald Reagan disagreed. In his farewell address at the White House nine days before he left office, the fortieth president said, "There's a clear cause and effect here that is as neat and predictable as a law of physics: as government expands, liberty contracts." William Saletan, a columnist for *Slate*, dubbed this observation, "Reagan's Law." The day after Reagan died, in 2004, Saletan recalled that statement: "This is what Reagan did best: He clarified the clash of ideas. He forced people to take sides. If you agreed with him, you were conservative. If you didn't, you weren't."

Hear, hear!

Saletan, unfortunately, didn't agree with him. "If liberty is the right to make a decent living or attend a good school, then getting government out of the way will suffice," he argued. "But if liberty is the ability to make a decent living or attend a good school, then getting government out of the way isn't enough. In fact, government expansion, in the form of student loans or job training, may be necessary."[1]

Or as one might put it today, if liberty is the right to use contraceptives, then getting government out of the way may suffice. But if liberty is the ability to get contraceptives for free while enrolled at Georgetown University's law school, then getting government out of the way isn't enough. In fact, government expansion, in the form of the HHS contraception mandate or Obamacare, may be necessary.

In his prescient book *They Only Look Dead*—which argued that things were not as bad for liberals and progressives as they seemed in the aftermath of the 1994 elections—the columnist E. J. Dionne argued that liberty isn't about big or small government. It's about the character of the government.

It's not the size, but how you use it.

A government that administers a large welfare system and exacts high taxes but provides strong protections for personal liberties and free expression would, in Dionne's telling, be freer than a military dictatorship that jails and tortures dissidents while providing few government services and levying lower taxes. Would you rather live, he might ask, in Pinochet's Chile, where the regime followed the free-market economic advice of Milton Friedman but where political dissenters "disappeared," or a nice welfare state like Canada with its single-payer health care system?

Reasonable persons may differ about where exactly Canada belongs on the scale of economic and political freedom (indeed, some parts of Canada may enjoy more economic freedom than the United States). But the chief lesson of the twentieth century, from the Soviet Union to China to Cuba, is that governments that assume comprehensive responsibility for citizens' material welfare tend to oppress them just as comprehensively.

Fortunately, the extremes that Dionne posits don't exhaust the possibilities. A police state would have to spend at least enough to support the military and security forces necessary to oppress the people, especially in case they ever decided to rebel. As nominally-communist China is learning, a tyranny cannot afford to allow the level of free communication and personal movement necessary for optimally functioning markets—something has to give. The connection between economic and political freedom, moreover, helps those who enjoy the former to obtain more of the latter.

Historically, the United States has afforded its citizens a high level of economic *and* political freedom. These freedoms are integral to the character of the government designed by the Founding Fathers, but they can be threatened as that government grows in size. In a country as large and diverse as the United States, if government grows beyond a certain point, it will lose its republican character. That's why big government matters—and must be stopped.

Gerald Ford was fond of the cliché, "A government big enough to give you everything you want is a government big enough to take away everything you have." The point isn't that the same government that gives poor people subsidized cheese will soon steal their lunchmeat. It's that government spending restricts your choices in all kinds of ways. Soon the beneficiaries of the government's largesse may be subject to the terms and conditions set by government. What big government gives, it can also take away.

THE NANNY WILL SEE YOU NOW

Let's consider an issue where size clearly mattered. In 2012, Mayor Michael Bloomberg of New York proposed restricting the sale of sodas and other sugary beverages to sixteen ounces. Don't like the idea? Tough, says Bloomberg. "Is purchasing two 16 oz sodas too much of an inconvenience to help reverse a national health catastrophe?," America's nanny asked on Twitter. It did not occur to him that low-income individuals forced to buy two drinks will end up fatter at a higher price. "Families who typically share one large drink will no longer be able to do so and will definitely wind up paying more," said Elliot Hoff of New Yorkers for Beverage Choices, which is funded by the beverage industry.

Despite the public criticism, many public health experts praised Bloomberg's soda tyranny. "For more than a hundred years, the soda industry has had free rein, and for many years it was not a problem because people mostly drank in moderation," Michael Jacobson of the Center for Science in the Public Interest told ABC News. "Now container sizes have jumped and the marketing of these drinks—especially to adolescents—has exploded to more than $2 billion a year."[2]

Why is this anyone's business? Some believe that the government should be able to do pretty much whatever it wants, for our own good, of course. But I suspect the heterodox conservative writer David Frum, who praised Bloomberg's soda ban as "visionary," gets closer to the answer to why something like this isn't unthinkable. "How can I justify this mucking around in people's personal lives?" Frum asked. "My direct response is that the Centers for Disease

Control estimates that one-tenth of national healthcare expenditures are spent to repair the health consequences of obesity. That's about $100 billion a year, not chump change."[3] "Slowing the rising rates of obesity in this country by just 1 percent a year over the next two decades would slice the costs of health care by $85 billion," reported National Public Radio.[4] *USA Today* cited a study claiming that merely keeping obesity rates flat would save half a trillion dollars by 2030.

In other words, it's not just about public health—it's about money. And in the age of Obamacare, the more your health care is provided at taxpayer expense, the more the rest of us will have to say about the personal choices that affect your health.

It's what Paul Hsieh, writing in *Forbes*, called "the dangerous synergy between the nanny state and universal health care." Japan measures the waistlines of citizens between the ages of forty and seventy-five. Men with a girth in excess of 33.5 inches and women over 35.4 inches may be forced to undergo counseling and their employers may be subject to sanctions. Norway taxes sugar and chocolate, Switzerland and Austria ban trans fats—as New York City, with great fanfare, has done for over five years. Massachusetts was considering a ban on school bake sales until popular protests shamed state legislators into silence.

Hsieh quotes G. K. Chesterton: "The free man owns himself. He can damage himself with either eating or drinking; he can ruin himself with gambling. If he does he is certainly a damn fool, and he might possibly be a damned soul; but if he may not, he is not a free man any more than a dog."[5]

That's not to say that Bloomberg's soda-size restrictions will reduce either costs or obesity. "It's never been definitively shown that the obesity epidemic is due to drinks larger than 16 ounces," Nikhil Dhurandhar, an obesity researcher from Pennington Biomedical

Research Center in Louisiana, told ABC. "It's like digging a hole in water. If you take away one thing, it's likely to be replaced."[6] In fact, the Centers for Disease Control has found no definitive link between soda consumption and obesity. Even if there were a link, there are enough loopholes to make the entire project ridiculous. Businesses that receive a "letter grade" from the city council were to be affected by the ban but not 7-Eleven, which could continue to sell its Big Gulp.

There have been bans on smoking in bars and restaurants for several years, of course, and the world hasn't come to an end. The real precedent for the anti-obesity crusade, however, isn't restrictions on smoking. It's the earlier health-and-morals-based attempt to eliminate the consumption of alcohol in America. Like its cousin, the federal war on drugs, the "Noble Experiment" of Prohibition ended in ignoble failure. It ought to be a cautionary tale for government busybodies, but they're unlikely to heed it.

Prohibition itself might stage a comeback. Some of the same activists who complain about sugary sodas have turned their watchful eyes toward the caloric content of alcoholic beverages. The author of a Centers for Disease Control study titled "Calories Consumed from Alcoholic Beverages by Young Adults, 2007–10," told the *New York Times*, "I think sometimes people forget completely that alcoholic beverages have calories."[7] "In New York City, it was smart to start with sugary drinks," Margo Wootan of the Center for Science in the Public Interest said to the *Boston Globe*. "Let's see how it goes and then think about next steps." Is Michael Bloomberg at the forefront of a new temperance movement?

One need not completely reject a government role in public health or believe that all lifestyle choices are equally healthy or valid to see a slippery slope here. Let's return to David Frum. "Suppose I said we have a huge problem with teen pregnancy," he wrote. "It causes poverty, increases the welfare bill, etc. If I urged a big federal abstinence-promotion program to deal with it, my conservative credentials would go unquestioned." Indeed, there *are* social welfare costs imposed by teen pregnancy and out-of-wedlock births. This was rightly one of the premises behind welfare reform in the 1990s. But the more our lives are subsidized by government, the more say government has over our lifestyles. Our choices come at the expense of everyone else, whether it is drinking an extra scotch every night, eating a Big Mac, smoking a cigarette, or quaffing a twenty-ounce Mountain Dew. My waistline, my lungs, and my heart are now your problem.

So much for the slogan "my body, my choice."

There will always be inconsistencies, of course. Even if it could be established beyond a reasonable doubt that there is a link between abortion and breast cancer—and there are doubts—Bloomberg is unlikely to back restrictions on abortion on the same public health grounds he restricts soda purchases.

But what if a differently motivated government came into power at the local, state, or federal level? It could argue quite plausibly that a lot of sexual choices burden taxpayers just as heavily as obesity does. Queens city councilman Daniel Halloran called Bloomberg's soda restrictions "absolutely ridiculous, unenforceable, and hypocritical.... What will they be telling me next?" he asked. "What time I should go to bed? How many potato chips I can eat? How big my steak should be?"[8] Why not? Unless we are free men and women, rather than dogs.

THE FOOD PYRAMID VS. THE CONSTITUTION

In June 2010, there was an opening on the Supreme Court. John Paul Stevens, dean of the liberal justices, had retired. President

Obama nominated his solicitor general, Elena Kagan, to replace him.

Since the Democratic ambush of Robert Bork in 1987 and the graphic saga of Clarence Thomas and Anita Hill in 1991, these nomination fights have become the political equivalent of mortal combat. George W. Bush was forced by members of his own party to withdraw the nomination of Harriet Miers after conservatives raised questions about her qualifications and judicial philosophy. The nation's highest court is closely divided between liberal and conservative justices.

Because we were simply trading one liberal justice for another, the Kagan nomination wasn't especially contentious. Obama also had the luxury of tapping her before the midterm elections, so he still enjoyed a nearly three-fifths Democratic majority in the Senate. Nevertheless, the Kagan confirmation hearings provided an opportunity to discuss controversial legal and constitutional questions— at least insofar as judicial nominees these days ever deign to answer them. One particularly instructive exchange took place between Kagan and Senator Tom Coburn, the conservative Oklahoma Republican.

Noting the artful evasions in Kagan's testimony, Coburn told her that she should be on *Dancing with the Stars*. Then he asked her a pointed question: "If I wanted to sponsor a bill, and it said, Americans, you have to eat three vegetables and three fruits every day, and I got it through Congress, and that's now the law of the land, got to do it, does that violate the Commerce Clause?"

"Sounds like a dumb law," Kagan replied, reasonably enough.

"Yeah, I got one that's real similar to it that I think is equally dumb," Coburn retorted with a not-too-thinly veiled reference to the individual mandate imposed by Obamacare. "I'm not going to mention which one it is."

Coburn and Kagan then began a delicate *pas de deux* about the Interstate Commerce Clause of Article I, Section 8, of the Constitution:

> *Kagan*: I think that the question about whether it is a dumb law is different from the question of whether it's constitutional. And I think the courts would be wrong to strike down laws that they think are senseless just because they're senseless.
>
> *Coburn*: Well, I guess the question I'm asking you is: Do we have the power to tell people what they have to eat every day?
>
> *Kagan*: Senator Coburn, um....
>
> *Coburn*: I mean, what is the extent of the Commerce Clause? We have this wide embrace of the Commerce Clause, which these guys who wrote this [*The Federalist Papers*] never ever fathomed that we would be so stupid to take away our liberties away by expanding the Commerce Clause this way.[9]

Bear in mind that Kagan was ascending to the Supreme Court from her perch as the top litigator in the Obama administration. Her job as solicitor general was to defend her boss's policies in court. Articulating a limiting principle for the Commerce Clause that is both meaningful and accommodates the individual mandate proved such an arduous task for Kagan's successor, Donald Verrilli, when he argued Obamacare's constitutionality before the Supreme Court, that he was widely compared to the bumbling lawyer in the comedy *My Cousin Vinny*. Kagan was much smoother. She didn't *duck* the question, insisted *Politico*'s Josh Gerstein; she suggested that our diets are among the non-economic activities not traditionally subject to congressional regulation under the Commerce Clause. The nominee also gave a perfunctory nod to the "substantial deference due to political branches" when evaluating even "ridiculous-sounding" laws.[10]

But what about the non-activity of not purchasing health insurance or any other product? Coburn amended his question to make it more germane to the challenge posed by the Affordable Care Act. "What if I said that eating three fruits and three vegetables would cut health care costs 20 percent?" he asked. "Now, we're into commerce. And since the government pays 65 percent of all the health care costs, why isn't that constitutional?"

"I feel as though the principles that I've given you are the principles that the court should apply," Kagan said simply.

This admittedly academic exchange about an improbable case illustrates an important problem. We have strayed so far from the doctrine of enumerated powers, which limits congressional authority to the small number of subjects listed in Article I, Section 8, of the Constitution, that the federal government is in principle unlimited. The defenders of this status quo, who believe the Constitution allows laws that would have been inconceivable to its framers or its ratifying public, cannot square their policies with anything other than an open-ended Constitution—a living document that is in fact a dead letter.

And so we return full-circle to Bloomberg. If our dietary choices have a substantial effect on health-care costs, which we all pay through our taxes, then why not regulate those choices? What if our failure to eat enough fruits and vegetables can be shown to overburden Medicare and Medicaid, which both face serious financial problems?

The New York Board of Health eventually approved Bloomberg's proposed soda regulations. Maybe the size of government matters after all.

SIN TAXES

Laws like Obamacare may lead to government interference with how you feed your body, but surely the government won't interfere with how you feed your soul. Right? Sadly, that does not seem to be the case. Government-run health care opens new doors for politicians and bureaucrats to police all sorts of lifestyle choices—all in the name, it turns out, of choice!

In addition to picking up the tab for a large portion of the country's health-care costs, Obamacare requires the government to decide what health benefits employers must provide. The law's patchwork of mandates, regulations, and subsidies on the existing employer-provided, private health insurance system invite the government to poke its nose into what kind of medical care private insurance plans will cover.

The most polarizing example of this new federal power is the Department of Health and Human Services' contraception mandate, a regulation even many Obamacare supporters never anticipated. Nancy Pelosi was right. We really did have to pass the legislation to find out what's in it.

What is the HHS mandate? It is quite simply an edict from the federal government that virtually all employers, including the vast majority of religious ones, must cover all forms of contraception regardless of individual or institutional conscience—even if none of the employees want such coverage.

"Today the department is announcing that the final rule on preventive health services will ensure that women with health insurance coverage will have access to the full range of the Institute of Medicine's recommended preventive services, including all FDA-approved forms of contraception," decreed HHS Secretary Kathleen Sebelius on January 20, 2012, exactly three years after Obama's first inauguration. "Women will not have to forgo these services because of expensive co-pays or deductibles, or because an insurance plan doesn't cover contraceptive services," Sebelius continued. "This rule is consistent with the laws in a majority of states which already require contraception coverage in health plans, and includes the exemption in the interim final rule allowing certain religious organizations not to provide contraception coverage." Employers that do not comply with this mandate will face heavy fines.[11]

HHS stipulated that by August 2012, all government-approved health plans—except for those paid for by "certain religious organizations"—would have to provide contraceptive services "without cost-sharing." That means for free. But paid for by whom?

The other problem was that the Obama administration's definition of "religious organizations" excluded a large majority of religious schools, charities, and non-profit organizations across the country. To qualify, a religious institution must "primarily" employ and serve "persons who share its religious tenets." It must also be devoted to the "inculcation of religious values as its purpose."

But what about feeding the hungry, clothing the naked, or taking care of the sick, as, say, Jesus might recommend? How about visiting prisoners, educating children, and working for justice? These are all "religious values" and "tenets" just as surely as is participating in a worship service. And why, in a pluralistic society, should a religious institution be penalized for serving those outside the faith? Should soup kitchens have to ask for a profession of faith before handing out sandwiches?

The Union of Orthodox Jewish Congregations of America highlighted the absurdity of these criteria:

> Most troubling, is the Administration's underlying rationale for its decision, which appears to be a view that if a religious entity is not insular, but engaged with broader

society, it loses its "religious" character and liberties. Many faiths firmly believe in being open to and engaged with the broader society and our fellow citizens of other faiths. The Administration's ruling makes the price of such an outward approach the violation of an organization's religious principles.[12]

Or as First Lady Michelle Obama memorably said at an African Methodist Episcopal Church service, "Our faith journey isn't just about showing up on Sunday. It's about what we do Monday through Saturday as well...."

"The defenders of the HHS mandate note that it protects freedom of worship, which indeed it does," observed Ross Douthat in the *New York Times*. "But a genuine free exercise of religion, not so much."[13]

After delaying the implementation of the mandate for religious employers by one year, the Obama administration floated a purported compromise. If a religious organization objects to the mandated coverage, the organization's insurance company must offer that coverage directly to the organization's employees, supposedly at the insurance company's own expense. The administration's concession is illusory for two reasons. First, insurance companies will simply raise the premiums of religious employers whose employees must receive the "free" contraceptives. The employer pays one way or another. Second, many of the larger religious employers, like universities and hospitals, are self-insured. There is no insurance company to do their dirty work. Obama's "compromise" solves nothing, writes Yuval Levin, because "the choice for religious employers is still between paying an insurer to provide their workers with access to a product that violates their convictions or paying a fine to the government."[14]

Yet many people don't understand what's at stake here, perhaps because moral qualms about contraception aren't as widely shared among the American public as objections to abortion. Here's how one commenter—on a conservative blog, no less—summarized the argument against the contraception mandate. "If an employer is concerned that employees will use their salary or benefits for something the employer doesn't approve of, they should be able to do something about that," the commenter wrote. "Elsewise, the religious liberty hath been trampled upon."

How cute thou art.

But the question isn't how an employee will spend his or her own hard-earned money. It is how the employer will spend its. Declining to spend it exactly as any given employee might wish, in the absence of any contractual agreement, isn't coercive. Telling the employer how it must spend its money is. Allowing a Catholic school to decline to subsidize the morning-after pill, in other words, isn't the same as overturning the *Griswold* decision invalidating anti-birth control laws.

In a past life, I worked for a marketing company that served Fortune 100 clients. I had a fairly generous health plan: eye care, dental coverage, numerous preventive options. When I went into journalism and worked for magazines—some of them underfunded and supported by small, struggling non-profits—my health benefits were, shall we say, somewhat less generous. But I never thought to inquire about my new employers' moral views about root canals or felt that they were somehow forbidding me to seek out a dentist. I understood the benefits to be part of the compensation package for working there, just as when I negotiated my salary.

Under Obamacare, the federal government will become intimately involved in such decisions. The delicate area where religion, morality, and human sexuality intersect is simply a bad place for the government to be. Moreover, the HHS mandate is simply foolish policy. "Insurance," says the financial commentator Peter Schiff, "is about things that are expensive and not likely to happen. Birth control isn't expensive and it's gonna happen." There are many other ways to expand access to contraception—making it available over the counter, for example—that do not implicate people who object to it as matter of conscience or impose the cost on third parties at all.

No one should have been surprised by the crimped view of religious freedom underlying the contraception mandate. After all, this was the same administration that decided it had a constitutional prerogative to be involved in churches' hiring and firing of their own ministers. A school affiliated with the Lutheran Church-Missouri Synod invested a teacher with the title of "Minister of Religion." After she was found to have violated the rules of the church, she was fired. Obama's Equal Employment Opportunity Commission (EEOC) sued the school to force it to rehire the teacher.

The case came before the Supreme Court as *Hosanna-Tabor Evangelical Lutheran Church and School v. EEOC*. Churches had generally been granted a "ministerial exception" from federal employment-discrimination laws as part of their First Amendment protections. To the astonishment of constitutional scholars of every perspective, the Obama administration argued that the court should repudiate the ministerial exception and treat churches no differently from secular employers. The Supreme Court—even the two liberals whom Obama himself had appointed—declined the president's invitation to trample on religious freedom and ruled unanimously against the EEOC.

The niceties of the First Amendment, however, did not trouble the secretary of Health and Human Services as she prepared to vindicate the reproductive rights of the employees of hospitals and parochial schools. Sebelius admitted under questioning by Congress that she had consulted no religious liberty cases before promulgating the contraception mandate.

Traditionally—and, since 1993, legally, under the Religious Freedom Restoration Act—the government has had to show a compelling interest to override religious conscience, and then it must pursue that interest by the least coercive means. The HHS mandate doesn't come close to satisfying those criteria.

REAGAN WAS RIGHT

The overweening power of government, in William Saletan's view, is merely the helping hand of a kindly big brother:

> For too many Americans, captivity is the inability to pay bills, save money, or go to college. For too many, the local tyrant is a company or religious majority. Government can impose worse captivity or become a greater tyrant, but not with the predictability of a law of physics. Liberty doesn't necessarily contract as government expands. Sometimes, you need more government to get more liberty.[15]

The problem is that when government pays your bills, sends you to college, or shields you from the censure of religious neighbors, it impinges on the liberty of someone else. That is why these are not *liberties* properly understood.

This same confusion is apparent in Franklin Roosevelt's "Four Freedoms," which Norman Rockwell immortalized in a famous series of paintings: freedom of speech, freedom of worship, freedom from fear, and freedom from want. The first two are negative rights, consistent with the Bill of Rights in the U.S. Constitution, and can be shared equally. The second two are positive rights that can in no way be shared equally and are difficult even to define.

"'Positive rights' trump freedom. According to this doctrine, human beings by nature owe, as a matter *of enforceable obligation*, part or even all of their lives to other persons," writes the libertarian theorist Tibor Machan. "If positive rights are valid, then negative rights cannot be, for the two are mutually exclusive."[16]

Under a system of negative rights, my right to obtain contraceptives cannot violate your right to freely exercise your religious beliefs or retain your earnings. Under a system of positive rights, it can. You don't have to go quite as far as Machan does to realize that the decision to provide certain services through the government may be meeting needs, but is not necessarily expanding liberty. That's not to say there are never reasons to expand government or to give up liberty in exchange for other goods. But we should at least honestly acknowledge the trade-offs involved rather than renaming every conceivable benefit a "liberty " or a "freedom."

Finally, a free society and a free economy eventually produce the wealth that will enable more people to pay their bills, get an education, and pursue happiness on their own terms, without violating the rights—or constricting the liberties—of others.

As government grows beyond its constitutional boundaries, it really does devour freedom.

CHAPTER SIX

THE AXIS OF BIG

When the late conservative media entrepreneur Andrew Breitbart launched a new constellation of websites to keep track of various pernicious forces in our national life, he put the adjective "big" in their titles: Big Hollywood, Big Journalism, Big Peace, and, of course, Big Government. It probably wasn't Breitbart's intention, but these names illustrate an uncomfortable truth in American politics: all the "bigs" travel together.

Most people understand that big labor is an ally of big government. And unions weren't shy about their big role in electing Barack Obama and a Democratic Congress in 2008. Big labor openly cheered for Obama. "Led by a candidate with an uncommon ability to inspire hope, we reclaimed our country from those who are serving corporate interests and the privileged at the expense of everyone else," announced John Sweeney, then-president of the ten-million-member union federation AFL-CIO.[1]

LOOK FOR THE UNION LABEL

The union bosses put their money where their mouths were. Unions gave $58 million to congressional candidates in 2008, some 91 percent of which went to Democrats. Labor leaders then piled on another $44 million in independent expenditures for Obama. To put this number in perspective, the Republican National Committee spent about $53 million on John McCain's presidential campaign that fall.

Labor contributed over $100 million for the Democrats, and that's probably just a fraction of what was actually spent. The value of the organizational prowess and campaign elbow grease that the unions provided to the Democrats is hard to quantify.

Organized labor may have an uneasy relationship with business-men, but they understand as well as any capitalist the importance of getting a return on your investment. "Unlike in the past, instead of saying 'OK, we've elected you, now do what's right by us,' we are going to keep our machinery in place," the AFL-CIO's president Richard Trumka told Bloomberg News. "We are going to make sure that our interests are considered at the front of the parade."[2]

And why shouldn't they have expected that kind of payoff? Obama more or less promised it. "It's time we had a president who will stand up for working men and women by building an economy that rewards not just wealth, but work and the workers who create it," the Democratic nominee said in a Labor Day video message to union households. "It's time you had a president who honors orga-nized labor—who's walked on picket lines; who doesn't choke on the word 'union'; who lets our unions do what they do best and organize our workers; and who will finally make the Employee Free Choice Act the law of the land."[3]

When you see a well-funded Democratic candidate—as Obama surely was in both 2008 and 2012—look for the union label.

Big government boosts sagging union membership—indirectly, by promising to eliminate secret ballots organizing elections; and directly, by increasing the size of the public sector, whose unionized employees are increasingly the faces of organized labor. This symbiotic relationship is obvious to most Americans. It's also a challenge that fiscally conservative leaders are increasingly rising to meet.

Collective bargaining in the public sector is different than in the private sector. Government unions set up phone banks and get out the vote for their politicians. They then sit down with those same politicians to negotiate their compensation. The taxpayers, who bear the cost, are not represented at the table. "When government unions sit down with the politicians they put into office, the relationship is not adversarial," observes Patrick Buchanan, who is more sympathetic to organized labor than many conservatives. "It is . . . incestuous. And taxpayers must pay the cost of their cohabitation."[4]

We have reached the point where pension benefits and other commitments to public-sector unions are crowding out of state and local budgets the welfare and educational programs liberals claim to support.

When Scott Walker was elected governor of Wisconsin in 2010, the state faced large budget deficits. Walker proposed limiting pay increases for state workers and taking away the government unions' power to bargain collectively over health care and pensions. Then all hell broke loose. Teachers walked out of their classrooms, sometimes taking students with them. Protesters poured into Madison, comparing Walker to Mussolini, Hitler, and the recently deposed Egyptian dictator Hosni Mubarak. Thousands chanted outside the state capitol, while hundreds attempted to camp inside. Democratic senators fled the state to prevent a quorum, delaying the passage of the collective bargaining bill. When the unions and their allies could stall the inevitable no longer, they gathered signatures to force the governor into a recall election.

The election was a rematch with Walker's 2010 Democratic opponent, Milwaukee mayor Tom Barrett. Despite a massive union investment, Walker won by slightly more than his original margin of victory, taking 53 percent of the vote. President Obama refused to make a last-minute campaign swing on Barrett's behalf, perhaps sensing defeat was in the air.

Then the sky didn't fall when the collective bargaining reforms took effect, even in Barrett's Milwaukee. "Despite early criticism from city officials," the *Milwaukee Journal Sentinel* reported, "new figures show Milwaukee will gain more than it will lose next year from the state's controversial budget and budget-repair legislation."[5] The city projected it would save at least $25 million a year by not having to negotiate health-care benefits with public-sector unions, $11 million more than was lost to state cuts in aid to cities and towns. The possibility existed for the savings from the law to reach $36 million. "And so you understand why unions are in such a rush to hold recall elections before voters see the benefits of Wisconsin's new law," the *Weekly Standard*'s John McCormack concluded.[6]

Walker isn't alone. Governors Mitch Daniels in Indiana, Chris Christie in New Jersey, John Kasich in Ohio, and even the liberal independent Lincoln Chafee in Rhode Island have all begun to push back against big labor, with varying degrees of success. Governor Rick Snyder of Michigan—the belly of the union beast—triumphantly signed a right-to-work law at the end of 2012.

BIG GOVERNMENT, INC.

If the connection between big government and big labor is well known—and attacked with increasing effect—the nexus of big government and big business remains a well-kept secret. The two are usually seen as adversaries rather than allies. In fact, they are often friends and partners. Obama may rail against Wall Street, but his campaign coffers are filled with its cash. He may talk about closing tax breaks for "big oil" and "fat cats" who fly on corporate jets, but in practice he shovels bailouts, loan guarantees, and federal subsidies to well-connected businesses.

Corporate welfare faces limited opposition, even—perhaps especially—in the Republican Party. The GOP has seldom heeded the advice of Reagan's budget director David Stockman to attack weak claims, not weak claimants. But while some small businesses are crushed by taxes and regulations and imperiled by financial crises, the big boys enrich themselves from the stimulus program, cap-and-trade proposals, and even Obamacare.

The two biggest financial supporters of the campaign to enact Obamacare were, in fact, labor unions and the pharmaceutical industry. The unions, which would benefit from the growth of government, received waivers protecting them from the act's more burdensome provisions. Big pharma would benefit from having more consumers of their products, at taxpayer expense.

It's a cliché that politics makes strange bedfellows, but there is really nothing strange about it—big government, big labor, and big business are frequently in bed together. Who is missing from this love triangle? Just the taxpayer and the start-ups trying to compete honestly in the free market. And you can bet that the Constitution isn't the bedtime reading on the nightstand.

The politicians who yell loudest about corporate greed are usually the first to shovel tax dollars into the corporate maw. There are many places to look for the billions spent annually in corporate welfare. But the innocuous-sounding crusade for "green energy" is as good a place as any to start.

IT'S NOT EASY BEING GREEN

In September 2010, Jennifer Granholm, then the governor of Michigan, celebrated a brave new chapter in "America's clean energy future." A123 Systems had built a 291,000-square-foot plant for manufacturing electric-car batteries in Livonia, Michigan, and the second-term Democrat was on hand for the grand opening. Granholm called it "a powerful demonstration of the job-creating potential of clean energy" and a "success story" of the $800 billion federal stimulus package. "You can see the pride in the faces of A123's workers and hear it in their voices," Granholm burbled in the *Huffington Post*. "They know they're helping shape our nation's clean energy future, and leading Michigan's economic recovery. Half of the new hires at A123's Livonia facility were previously unemployed."[7]

A report by the Mackinac Center for Public Policy paints a less rosy picture. "[T]he company has laid off 125 employees and had a net loss of $172 million through the first three quarters of 2011.... Yet, [in February 2012] A123's Compensation Committee approved a $30,000 raise for [Chief Financial Officer David] Prystash just days after Fisker Automotive [, which was to be A123's main customer and in which it had invested $23 million,] announced the U.S. Energy Department had cut off what was left of its $528.7 million loan it had previously received."

Despite A123's financial woes, other executives also reaped the rewards of America's clean energy future. Mackinac reported, "Robert Johnson, vice president of the energy solutions group, got a 20.7 percent pay increase going from $331,250 to $400,000, while Jason Forcier, vice president of the automotive solutions group, saw his pay increase from $331,250 to $350,000."[8]

The federal government gave A123 $249.1 million in grant money through the Department of Energy, while the state of Michigan supplied another $141 million in tax credits and other subsidies. All told, that is $390 million in taxpayer dollars for a company that was losing money, shedding workers, and giving its bigwigs big paydays.

Fisker Automotive, the hybrid electric car manufacturer, bought lithium ion batteries from A123. Fisker had received $193 million from the feds before the Department of Energy decided the company wasn't doing well enough even for government work and terminated the rest of its $528.7 million loan guarantee.

A123 filed for Chapter 11 bankruptcy protection in October 2012. By the end of the year, it was announced—much to Congress's displeasure—that A123 was to be sold to a Chinese manufacturing company, Wanxiang Group. The significance of the firm's potentially moving to China wasn't lost on anyone.

"As with Solyndra and other failed 'green' firms, taxpayers already face a significant loss," complained Senator Lisa Murkowski, a Republican from Alaska. "The real irony is that these assets were developed in part with stimulus money that the federal government borrowed from countries such as China. So now," she continued, "not only do we have to pay that money back, we have also lost the technology we spent it on in the first place." That's a far cry from the scenario outlined by Granholm, now a television host and slightly manic Democratic convention speaker.

"It is exceedingly frustrating to stand by and watch the fruits of our taxpayer-funded research and development get shipped overseas to a Chinese firm," added Representative Paul Broun, a Republican from Georgia. "It is a dirty cycle: We borrow money from China, use it to fund R&D in America, and then watch as the benefits of that research are reaped on foreign soil."[9]

GREEN IS BLUE

The most famous green-energy public-private partnership of the Obama era is, of course, Solyndra. Thanks to this boondoggle, it's no longer a secret that these schemes often leave employees out of work and taxpayers holding the bag while investors get rich and politicians get campaign funds. Solyndra received a $573 million loan guarantee from the federal government—Obama's first major "public investment" in alternative energy. The White House originally estimated that government support would help Solyndra create four thousand new jobs. But by September 2011, the company had largely ceased operations, filed for Chapter 11 bankruptcy protection, and laid off nearly all its employees. The U.S. taxpayer is on the hook to pay back the loan.

When governments try to invest in emerging industries, they often swing and miss. Politicians and bureaucrats don't have the same batting average as the free market. But there is another problem inherent in such government interventions: the public largesse inevitably accrues to the politically connected. Solyndra's case was no different.

George Kaiser, an Oklahoma billionaire who just happened to be a bundler for Barack Obama's 2008 presidential campaign, owned roughly 35 percent of the company. Each Obama bundler raised at least $100,000. The more than $500 million loan guarantee wasn't just a random mistake, and Solyndra's fate was not an unpredictable fluke.

"The economic reality is that Solyndra loses money on every solar panel it sells," the Hoover Institution's Peter Schweizer wrote in his book *Throw Them All Out*. "The company has never been profitable. The plan was simple, and has become a pattern with other companies: secure government money, go public, and get out." A Solyndra investor memorably told the *Wall Street Journal*, "There was a perceived halo around the loan. If we get the loan, then we can definitely go public and cash out."[10]

And cash out they did. Kaiser and Solyndra's other investors will be paid back before the taxpayer. But the recipients of these loan guarantees and subsidies don't just get access to government money. Government backing serves almost like a *Good Housekeeping* seal of approval for other investors, helping businesses partially on the public dole raise more private capital as well.

"Crony capitalism" is the name given to corporate welfare for politically connected enterprises. But it has come to signify a broader departure from the free market in which profit remains private while losses are socialized. Incentives to self-regulate disappear. Uncle Sam is waiting in the wings to assume responsibility. This ugly distortion of capitalism predates the Obama administration. It undergirded the $700 billion Troubled Asset Relief Program—the bank bailout—and the 2005 energy bill, which gave Solyndra-style boondoggles their start. President George W. Bush signed both of these programs into law.

But by making green jobs and government investment in alternative energy such a large part of its economic stimulus strategy, the Obama administration is institutionalizing crony capitalism. There is no shortage of cronies. To cite just one example, Schweizer found that $16.4 billion out of $20.5 billion in loan guarantees under an Energy Department program went to companies run or primarily owned by Obama's financial backers. "Their political largesse is probably the best investment they ever made in alternative energy," Schweizer wrote. "It brought them returns many times over."

In some cases, the people running the loan programs are also financial supporters of Obama. The bundler Steve Spinner raised about $500,000 for Obama in 2008 and, according to a *Politico* report, has brought in roughly the same amount for the president's reelection effort. He was dubbed the campaign's "liaison to Silicon Valley." Spinner went from the Obama national finance committee to overseeing strategic operations for the Department of Energy's loan program.[11]

Spinner later left the administration for the Center for American Progress. His biography on the organization's website said he "helped oversee the more than $100 billion of loan guarantee and direct lending authority for the Title XVII Loan Guarantee Program and the Advanced Technology Vehicles Manufacturing loan program." (Spinner left the Center for American Progress in October 2011.) He became something of a household name when he was ensnared in the Solyndra debacle. The government released emails showing that Spinner, as the *Huffington Post* put it, "was more actively involved in a loan for Solyndra LLC than administration officials have acknowledged." According to the emails, Spinner pushed to have the Solyndra loan finalized before Vice President Joe Biden's planned trip to the company's Fremont, California, groundbreaking ceremony. "How hard is this? What is he waiting for?" Spinner complained. "I have the OVP [Office of the Vice President] and WH [White House] breathing down my neck on this. They are getting itchy to get involved."

The administration's line has always been that the White House didn't know the Solyndra investors' names and that Spinner wasn't involved in the approval process for the loans. These emails, released to the House Energy and Commerce Committee as well as the media, aren't exactly proof of the contrary, but they don't suggest dispassion or neutrality either.

Solyndra wasn't the only cozy green-energy deal. The Department of Energy also gave a $737 million loan guarantee to a company called SolarReserve, a partner with Pacific Global Group, which in turn employs Nancy Pelosi's brother-in-law Ronald as a high-ranking executive.

BLOWIN' IN THE WIND

The St. Louis-based wind energy firm Wind Capital received a $107 million tax break. Wind Capital's current chairman, former president, and CEO is Tom Carnahan—son of the former Missouri governor Mel Carnahan and the former U.S. senator Jean Carnahan, brother of Congressman Ross Carnahan and Missouri secretary of state Robin Carnahan, and, for good measure, Obama's chief fundraiser in the Show Me State. "It's increasingly hard to tell the government's green jobs subsidies apart from the Democrats' friends and family rewards program," cracked the *Weekly Standard*'s Mark Hemingway.[12] Perhaps they might feel differently about this largesse if Haliburton got into the green jobs act.

Then there is the curious case of Abound Solar, a Colorado-based supplier of advanced-technology solar electric panels tied to the medical-device heiress and Democratic donor Patricia Stryker. The Department of Energy approved $400 million in federal loan guarantees for Abound. President Obama and the former Colorado governor Bill Ritter applauded the move.

Abound promised to expand its operations within the state of Colorado and open a new plant in Indiana, creating some 1,500 jobs. Republicans also got into the act. Indiana's governor, Mitch Daniels, helped the company win twelve million dollars in state incentives, and some GOP members of Indiana's House delegation helped obtain the Energy Department loan guarantees. Abound also received a three-million-dollar development grant during the Bush administration.

Like Solyndra before it, Abound was soon bankrupt. According to the company's bankruptcy filings, net sales plummeted from twenty-six million dollars in 2010 to twenty-two million in 2011 and a paltry one million in 2012. Some four hundred jobs were lost in Colorado, the Indiana plant was never built, and the company defaulted on all its federal loans. The collapse of Abound occurred just seven months after it boasted of being the "anti-Solyndra." The Energy Department cut off the loan guarantees after about $70 million, just as the Solyndra scandal was reaching full bloom.

Abound's executives blamed China. "With over $30 billion in reported government subsidies, Chinese panel makers were able to sell below cost and put Abound out of business before we were big enough to pose a real competitive threat to China's rapidly growing market share," CEO Craig Witsoe stated in prepared congressional testimony.[13] Apparently, Abound just wasn't government-subsidized enough.

But Michael Bastasch reported in the *Daily Caller* that Abound Solar had bigger problems, the chief one being that it was selling a faulty product. "Our solar modules worked as long as you didn't put them in the sun," a company source admitted, later saying, "The DOE hurt us more than anything." Bastasch revealed that Abound "knew its panels were faulty prior to obtaining taxpayer dollars, according to sources, but kept pushing product out the door in order to meet Department of Energy goals required for their $400 million loan guarantee."[14]

Abound is also under investigation by the Weld County district attorney's office in Colorado for consumer and securities fraud. Company leaders have categorically denied any wrongdoing. "I never saw an instance where any material information, be it product information, technical information, financial information, whatever, was misrepresented to anybody, be it a customer, an investor, an employee, a banker, whatever," Abound's co-founder and former chairman, John Hill, told the *Denver Post*.[15]

What is not in dispute is that taxpayers are left footing the bill for between forty and sixty million dollars in losses. Private investors lost as much as $300 million. The green future was not what it was cracked up to be.

CORRUPTION ABOUNDS

What role did politics play in Abound Solar's trip to the federal trough? The billionaire Pat Stryker was the founder of Bohemian Companies, an early investor in Abound, and an Obama campaign bundler. According to the Center for Responsive Politics, she has donated more than $440,000 to Democratic candidates since the 2008 election cycle. Dubbed the "Colorado crony" by the *Washington Free Beacon*, Stryker was also active in the Colorado Democracy Alliance, a coalition of wealthy liberals who have worked the system of campaign finance reform laws to push the state toward the Democrats in recent elections.[16]

"[Stryker] is listed in the White House logs three times, and all of those times come around key points in the process of Abound Solar getting this loan," reported Todd Shepherd of the Independence Institute in a video detailing Stryker's and Abound's ties to the

Obama administration.[17] As in the Solyndra case, journalists obtained emails suggesting White House involvement in the loan guarantee decision. "You better [let] him know the [White House] wants to move Abound forward," wrote an Energy Department loan executive, Jonathan Silver, apparently complaining that a Treasury Department adviser did not schedule conference calls about Abound quickly enough.

Congress subsequently launched an investigation, demanding that Energy Secretary Steven Chu hand over documents about the loan guarantee. "The administration for too long has attempted to distance itself from the management of the program and its failures, embracing the ribbon-cutting ceremonies and photo ops, while blaming the bankruptcies and wasted taxpayer money on someone else," said Representative Darrell Issa, the California Republican who chairs the House Oversight and Government Reform Committee.

In February 2012, the *Washington Post* reported, "$3.9 billion in federal grants and financing flowed to 21 companies backed by firms with connections to five Obama administration staffers and advisers."[18] This includes Sanjay Wagle, a venture capitalist who headed Clean Tech for Obama in 2008. After the election, Wagle joined the Energy Department just as the administration was planning a round of government investments in the clean technology firms.

Over the next three years, the department spent $2.4 billion in public funds on clean energy companies in which Wagle's old firm, Vantage Point Venture Partners, had invested. The White House maintains that its venture capitalist advisers do not make these decisions, though some probes have found evidence of at least informal lobbying.

"To believe those quiet conversations don't happen in the hallways—about a project being in a certain congressman's district or being associated with a significant presidential donor—is naive," said David Gold, a venture capitalist who once worked at the Office of Management and Budget and who is critical of the administration's energy investments. He told the *Post*, "When you're putting this kind of pressure on an organization to make decisions on very big dollars, there's increased likelihood that political connections will influence things."

How could it be otherwise? Politicians have always done favors for supporters. Businesses have always spent money to try to influence the government. As the government's role in the economy grows, the influence of private interests on public policy will also grow, even when the people involved have honorable intentions.

Liberals are bedeviled by an embarrassing contradiction. They decry the role of money in politics—if you don't believe me, Google "Citizens United"—even as they press for public investments in private energy enterprises. Despite their sordid record, they steadfastly maintain that, as the *Washington Examiner*'s Timothy P. Carney puts it, "Conservative money is bad, and linked to greed, while liberal money is self-evidently philanthropic."[19] If your name happens to be Kennedy, your money obviously falls in the latter category. Robert Kennedy Jr. predicted in 2008 that Obama's energy policies would lead to a "Green Gold Rush,"[20] and he's getting a piece of the action. The environmental activist is a partner in BrightSource, a company that received $1.4 billion in loan guarantees to build the Ivanpah Solar Electric Generating System in California. Whatever the merits of this project may be, it's not philanthropy.

ABOUT THOSE JOBS . . .

Despite the president's confident assurances that public investment in renewable energy will create a multitude of high-wage jobs that can never be transferred overseas, the record remains a matter of considerable debate. A 2009 study by Gabriel Calzada, an economics professor at Juan Carlos University in Madrid, found that for every green job created with taxpayer money in Spain since 2001, 2.2 other jobs were destroyed. Worse, only a tenth of the new green jobs ended up being permanent.

An American report, "Green Jobs Myths," was published the same year. Its authors concluded that the special interests promoting green jobs programs often work from dubious assumptions bolstered by flawed economic analyses. One of the co-authors, Andrew Morriss, a professor of law and business at the University of Illinois, told me that green projects seldom include "net jobs calculations" and instead extrapolate from "very small base numbers." Morriss points out that the green studies tend to assume "very large multiplier effects" when "all the experience we have suggests that these multiplier effects are exaggerated or overstated."[21]

Other economists disagree, of course. But there's no question that these initiatives have included some spectacular failures. Consider the Chevrolet Volt. According to one estimate, taxpayers will shovel three billion dollars in government loans, subsidies, tax credits, rebates, and grants into the production of General Motors' electric car. $2.4 billion of that will come from federal funds, and the state of Michigan will contribute $690 million or so. "But even with spectacular deals like these, GM has so far only managed to sell about 8,000 of their vaunted Obamacars," writes Larry Bell in *Forbes*. (By comparison, Ford sold roughly 84,000 Edsels). "And despite another big gift we gave them in the form of a huge TARP bailout, the prognosis doesn't look good at all."[22] MIT's *Technology Review* characterizes it as "good news" when Fisker Automotive, the troubled electric car manufacturer, produces 1,500 cars and claims to have sold "hundreds."

General Electric's Shepherds Flat initiative in northern Oregon is another example of U.S. tax dollars gone with the wind. The Manhattan Institute's Robert Bryce has called it "America's worst wind-energy project."[23] Bryce notes that the Department of Energy has given GE and its partners a $1.06 billion loan guarantee for the project, and the *Wall Street Journal* reports that the Treasury Department will kick in a $490 million cash grant once the project is underway.

Since Shepherds Flat is expected to create only about thirty-five green jobs, the cash grant alone comes out to $16.3 million per job. and *Forbes*'s Bell quips that taxpayers may find that price tag "just a little steep." But Shepherds Flat has critics even within the Obama administration. An October 2010 memo attributed to energy policy czar Carol Browner and economic adviser Lawrence Summers, among others, complained that the project's backers had too "little skin in the game." Their investment was relatively small, the subsidy large, and the likely environmental benefit insufficient to justify the cost.

Crony capitalism has become an epithet on both the left and the right. Ralph Nader and Sarah Palin have condemned the practice. It's as unpopular at Tea Party rallies as in the campgrounds of Occupy Wall Street. "The American people do not like Friendly Fascism," wrote R. Emmett Tyrrell, Jr. in his book *The Death of Liberalism*. "They do not even like corporate cronyism." Yet it thrives.[24]

Most liberals still believe that targeted government investments in renewable energy and other emerging technologies are both environmentally sound and economically necessary. The government's collaboration with the big businesses they distrust—corporate bogeymen like GE and GM—seems not to bother them if someone has slapped a "green" label on the project. Similarly, many conservatives still confuse a reflexive defense of business—no matter how dependent on government a particular business may be—with the defense of free markets.

Boondoggles undertaken in the name of national security often attract insufficient scrutiny on the right, while boondoggles in the name of environmentalism get a pass from the left. Muddled thinkers across the political spectrum believe that the solution to crony capitalism is the further entanglement of government and business. As the *Wall Street Journal* put it, they want "capitalists to be more answerable to the politicians."[25]

Crony capitalism isn't an exclusively liberal sin. But it is built into the economic and environmental policies of the Obama administration, which liberals support at the expense of their ethical standards.

In pronouncing the Obama White House scandal-free, the columnist Jonathan Alter argued that the greening of crony capitalism doesn't count as a scandal. Tony Robinson, a political scientist in Colorado, agreed. Evaluating the odiferous Abound Solar affair, he shrugged, "If that's as bad as it gets, it's not very bad." He told a *Denver Post* reporter, "I don't see any evidence of systematic corruption."

To borrow a phrase from the late Daniel Patrick Moynihan, this seems like defining corruption down. And defining capitalism down, too.

CHAPTER SEVEN

OBAMACARE'S UNIQUE THREAT

The Patient Protection and Affordable Care Act—affectionately known as "Obamacare"—didn't set up a single-payer health-care system like Canada's. It did not create a federal agency on quite the same scale as the British National Health Service. In order to get Obamacare through Congress, its supporters could not even include the "public option"—a government-run health agency that would allegedly compete with private health insurance. This exclusion rankled many Obamacare supporters, including the single-payer advocates for whom the public option already *was* a compromise.

Paul Krugman wrote from his perch at the *New York Times*:

> Remember, to make reform work we have to have an
> individual mandate. And everything I see says that there
> will be a major backlash against the idea of forcing people
> to buy insurance from the existing companies. That back-
> lash was part of what got Obama the nomination! Having
> the public option offers a defense against that backlash.[1]

Krugman ultimately concluded that one of the best things about the
public option was simply that it would be run by the government:
"[S]ooner or later Democrats have to take a stand against Reagan-
ism—against the presumption that if the government does it, it's
bad."[2]

The absence of a public option, an expansion of Medicare to
people under sixty-five, and a single-payer system are frequently
cited as proof that the president's signature legislation wasn't a big
government project. Some even argue that it is a free-market reform.
"[T]he new health-care-reform law passed in March is an entirely
private-insurer, free-market-based reform," the *Economist* reported
in May 2010. "If someone were to refer to it as a 'government takeover of the health-care sector', that person would hold a factually
incorrect ideological belief."[3] In fact, the *Economist* went on to
compare such a belief with fevered 9/11 conspiracy theories and the
suspicion that Barack Obama was born outside the United States.
More than a report about health-care reform, the *Economist* story
began by wrestling with the problem of "how to keep Americans
from believing political falsehoods."

Thanks.

Remember that we are discussing a law that expands Medicaid—
a government health-care program—while adding new government
health exchanges, subsidies, regulations, price controls, and mandates

on both individuals and employers. Private insurers will be heavily regulated and heavily subsidized, participating in government-managed competition to sell their newly government-mandated product. There will remain a larger private component to the health-care sector in the earliest phases of Obamacare than exists in some other industrialized democracies. But the plan was still a large expansion of the size, cost, and scope of the federal government's involvement in health care—a role that could well continue to grow over time. But to liberals, because somebody other than the government is still making money, Obamacare qualifies as a free-market health-care reform.

BUILDING OBAMACARE

The enactment of Obamacare in 2010 was both a stunning victory for the supporters of big government and the result of a horrible miscalculation by its opponents.

That is *not* to say, as some maintain, that the Republicans did not do enough to negotiate with the Obama administration and the congressional Democrats as the bill was being written. "At the beginning of this process we made a strategic decision: unlike, say, Democrats in 2001 when President Bush proposed his first tax cut, we would make no deal with the administration," David Frum wrote in the *Daily Beast*. "No negotiations, no compromise, nothing. We were going for all the marbles.... This time, when we went for all the marbles, we ended with none."[4]

This seems like a misreading. First of all, Democrats held three-fifths majorities in both houses of Congress for most of the Obamacare debate. That included a filibuster-proof majority in the Senate, until Scott Brown won his special election in early 2010. Democrats reacted to Brown's election by ramming the bill through the Senate by means of "reconciliation," a legislative process intended for budget bills, which prevented a Republican filibuster.

President Obama didn't need any Republican votes. Certainly, he would have liked some, to provide a bit of bipartisan cover and spread the political risk. But in the end, he wasn't even willing to negotiate on abortion funding, which cost him his sole Republican supporter in the House.

With such large congressional majorities, the fate of Obamacare—like the fate of Hillarycare before it—was always going to hinge on the politics of the Democratic caucus. Could they produce a bill that went far enough for liberals yet could win enough votes from moderates from reddish and purple districts to pass?

Negotiations with Republicans almost certainly would have strengthened the bargaining posture of the liberals in the Democratic caucus because they, not the centrists, would have been the swing vote deciding whether or not the bill was passed. The Congressional Progressive Caucus was reluctant to compromise on things such as the public option in order to win the votes of Joe Lieberman or Ben Nelson. How much would they have been willing to compromise to win the vote of Charles Grassley? Probably not much. In that context, curtailing the Medicaid expansions would have looked like an unpardonable capitulation by the White House, which is why it was never likely to happen.

With Nancy Pelosi's blessing, the House passed a version of Obamacare that contained an amendment by Representative Bart Stupak, a pro-life Democrat from Michigan, imposing a fairly airtight ban on abortion funding. The Stupak amendment was aimed at a small group of wavering pro-life Democrats, not at Republicans. In fact, the amendment won over only one Republican vote, a freshman representing an overwhelmingly Democratic New Orleans district. Liberals eventually succeeded in removing the Stupak amendment. If it had been part of negotiations with Republicans, a full-blown liberal revolt would have been unavoidable.

Unanimous Republican opposition strengthened the hand of centrist Democrats because Obama could afford few defections. It was, in fact, these Democrats who defeated the public option, pushed for a lower price tag, and briefly got the House to exclude funds for elective abortion. The Republicans who had briefly been involved in the negotiations, by contrast, were open to the public option "trigger"—a feature to the left of the bill that ultimately passed.

A federal version of the plan that Governor Mitt Romney signed into law in Massachusetts—with exchanges, subsidies, and an individual mandate—was the most conservative bill that could have passed under the circumstances. To believe otherwise is to engage in wishful thinking.

PAVING THE WAY FOR OBAMACARE

But strategic miscalculations by Republicans and conservatives did pave the way for Obamacare in one important way: by refusing to unite around a bold free-market alternative, they ensured that the issue would ultimately be dealt with on liberal and Democratic terms. "Rather than make a prolonged case for health policy that does not involve endless expansion of entitlements and insurance subsidies," writes Peter Suderman, "the GOP has instead focused primarily on reacting to Democratic proposals."[5] That's a strategy that works only as long as no Democratic proposals pass. The Republican approach to health-care reform—abetted by far too many conservative journalists and policy wonks—has been to vacil-late between opposing Democratic plans and aping them.

Remember when Newt Gingrich, in his previously discussed Las Vegas health-care back-and-forth with Mitt Romney, said that he had embraced the individual mandate to stop Hillarycare? Back in 1994, the liberal Republican senator John Chafee of Rhode Island, a disciple of Nelson Rockefeller, was Bob Dole's point man for craft-ing a bill to preempt the Clinton health-care plan. Naturally, Chafee's proposal contained an individual mandate, which was thought to be less onerous to businesses than the employer mandate favored by the Clintons. Republicans embraced the talking point that this was similar to requiring drivers to carry automobile insurance. Most conservatives, however, both inside and outside Congress, did not support the Chafee-Dole proposal, and it was never a serious part of the Republican agenda. The Democrats had started a national conversation on the problems with the American health-care system, and Chafee-Dole was merely an attempt to have something to say. Once Hillarycare was safely defeated, the bill was shoved down the memory hole much like the health-care reform proposals of GOP presidential candidates from George H. W. Bush to John McCain.

Unfortunately, the individual mandate didn't die with Chafee-Dole. The idea percolated through conservative policy circles as far back as the late 1980s, pushed chiefly by Stuart Butler, a domestic policy expert at the Heritage Foundation. In 1991, Butler described the individual mandate as a way of heading off an employer mandate:

> We would include a mandate in our proposal—not a mandate on employers, but a mandate on heads of house-holds—to obtain at least a basic package of health insur-ance for themselves and their families. That would have to include, by federal law, a catastrophic provision in the

form of a stop loss for a family's total health outlays. It would have to include all members of the family, and it might also include certain very specific services, such as preventive care, well baby visits, and other items.[6]

The *Wall Street Journal*'s James Taranto acknowledges that Butler's proposal was less sweeping than Obamacare's individual mandate and was more focused on catastrophic care. But it represented a huge concession in principle. "... Butler's vague language—'it might also include certain very specific services ... and other items'—would seem to leave the door wide open for limitless expansion," he warns. "Whatever the particular differences, the Heritage mandate was indistinguishable *in principle* from the ObamaCare one. In both cases, the federal government would force individuals to purchase a product from a private company—something that Congress has never done before."

Taranto worked at Heritage at the time its analysts were formulating their version of the individual mandate. He watched the idea circulate among Beltway conservatives and finally gain a foothold in their most influential think tank. But the proposal never had much support from grassroots conservatives. Taranto discusses the contradiction:

> Heritage did put forward the idea of an individual mandate, though it predated HillaryCare by several years. We know this because we were there: In 1988–90, we were employed at Heritage as a public relations associate (a junior writer and editor), and we wrote at least one press release for a publication touting Heritage's plan for comprehensive legislation to provide universal "quality, affordable health care."[7]

But for Hillarycare, I doubt that a substantial number of congressional Republicans would have ever dabbled in the individual mandate. Even with Butler's mandate making the rounds in the conservative enclaves of the capital, proposals by conservatives like Senator Phil Gramm of Texas, Senator Don Nickles of Oklahoma, and Representative Cliff Stearns of Florida didn't make use of the idea.

Nevertheless, the seeds of Romneycare were planted. They would eventually blossom into Obamacare.

TED KENNEDY REPUBLICANS

Mitt Romney wasn't the only Republican who would join forces with Ted Kennedy on health care. Nor was Chafee-Dole the last time Republicans attempted a watered-down version of Democratic health-care reform proposals. In 1996, Senator Nancy Landon Kassebaum—a Kansas Republican whose father, Alf Landon, was the GOP nominee for president in 1936—paired with Kennedy to advance a bill that sought to increase the portability of health insurance between jobs and to limit insurer exclusions for preexisting conditions. President Clinton signed Kennedy-Kassebaum into law, but the measure didn't solve the problems it was intended to address. Both were still issues when Obamacare was being debated thirteen years later.

Senator Orrin Hatch, the Utah Republican, then teamed up with Kennedy to create the State Children's Health Insurance Program (SCHIP). In response to the Mormon lawmaker's political fling with Kennedy, *National Review* branded Hatch a "latter-day liberal." That was about the only negative press Hatch received as a result of his health-care partnership. More typical was this enthusiastic write-up in *Time*:

No, it was nothing new last week when Republican Senator Orrin Hatch joined forces with archliberal Edward
Kennedy to introduce a piece of legislation.... Nor was it
shocking that Hatch, a conservative who led the defense
of Clarence Thomas and is the Senate's foremost advocate
of a balanced-budget amendment, wanted to lavish taxpayer money on vulnerable children. A grandfather 17
times over, Hatch has often championed laws that expand
day care and fund child-nutrition programs.

The magazine dubbed the Hatch-Kennedy effort "the only major
piece of legislation to emerge from a do-little Congress this year."

"No wonder Senate majority leader Trent Lott was so furious,"
Time's James Carney continued. "Instead of working with his leadership to produce a Republican proposal, Hatch devised a bipartisan
bill with Kennedy that Republicans will be hard pressed to oppose."[8]
That, of course, was precisely the problem for anyone interested in
a free-market alternative.

That's not to say that Hatch didn't receive any concessions. While
Kennedy-Kassebaum mostly expanded regulations, SCHIP spent
federal money in order to provide state governments with matching
funds to buy health insurance for families with children who earned
too much to qualify for Medicaid. It was a block grant rather than
an open-ended entitlement.

SCHIP, nevertheless, proved expensive. Federal spending on the
program doubled from 2001 to 2006. The Congressional Budget
Office found that some middle-class families had stopped paying
for their own insurance and passed the bill to Uncle Sam instead:
"Some parents who would have otherwise had family coverage
through their employer might decline it for their children—or might
decline coverage altogether—if their children are eligible for SCHIP."

When SCHIP came up for reauthorization in 2007, there were attempts to expand its coverage to people with even higher incomes. President Bush vetoed such measures twice, arguing that the original purpose of SCHIP was to help poor families, not grow into an ever-larger obligation.

Republicans faced an onslaught of bad press as a result of their efforts to contain SCHIP's growth. MSNBC's liberal commentator Rachel Maddow said, "This is a bill that expands private health insurance for poor kids and pays for it by raising the cigarette tax. Like, you can't make this a prettier bill unless you added puppies to it or something." The *Washington Post*'s Jeffrey Birnbaum claimed that the program's expansion was defeated by "the tobacco lobby and America's Health Insurance Plans [AHIP], the leading trade organization for health insurance companies."[9] AHIP was actually a consistent supporter of SCHIP expansion for the obvious reason that more government subsidies would encourage more people to buy their products. The industry group merely opposed a particular *version* of the proposal, which would have funded the expansion by cutting another subsidy to insurers rather than taxing "the tobacco lobby."

Puppies and everything nice ultimately prevailed, however. President Obama signed a bill expanding SCHIP during his first week in office. The pharmaceutical industry praised this move as a "tremendous victory for millions of low-income, uninsured American families, and, indeed, for all Americans." Like most presents from Washington, the program came "taxpayers not included."

The important lesson to learn from SCHIP expansion is that it did nothing to stop bigger government interventions like Obamacare. The president expanded the program and moved without a pause to the next stage of his federal health-care agenda.

Of course, Republicans had done nothing to stop health care from breaking the bank when they controlled the presidency and both houses of Congress. In fact, their one major piece of health-care legislation ended up costing vast sums of money and further weakening the case against future legislation like Obamacare. In 2000, both George W. Bush and Al Gore supported the addition of a prescription drug benefit to Medicare. The idea polled well, especially among seniors. Florida ended up being the state that decided the presidential election.

Bush proposed a benefit that was projected to cost less than the Democrats' version while containing some free-market features such as health savings accounts and no price controls. Earlier versions were supposed to provide incentives for obtaining private health insurance as part of qualifying for the drug coverage. But the prescription drug benefit that actually passed added between $8 trillion and $15.5 trillion to Medicare's already substantial unfunded liabilities. Not for nothing did former U.S. Comptroller General David Walker call the bill "the most fiscally irresponsible piece of legislation since the 1960s."

"It's important to remember that the congressional budget resolution capped the projected cost of the drug benefit at $400 billion over 10 years," Bruce Bartlett later wrote in *Forbes*.[10] Otherwise, the bill was vulnerable to a point of order under congressional rules. But Richard Foster, Medicare's chief actuary, believed it would cost more than $534 billion over the same time period.

Foster later alleged that a Republican appointee in the Health and Human Services Department had threatened to fire him if he blew the whistle on the prescription drug benefit's cost. Foster wasn't the only one whom the Republican leadership had to sway by extraordinary means. Michigan GOP Representative Nick Smith claimed that his colleagues had promised that his son would be guaranteed to succeed him in Congress if he voted for the bill. House Republican leaders had to extend the vote past the standard fifteen-minute window in order to enact the legislation. While some of these allegations are still contested, it is beyond dispute that the new benefit was entirely unfunded by new revenues or spending cuts. The Republicans' irresponsibility in passing the prescription drug benefit weakened their argument against Obamacare, which the Congressional Budget Office (rather implausibly) scored as deficit-neutral.

After the Clinton health-care plan was defeated in the 1990s, many Republicans seemed to think they would never have to face the issue again or that co-authoring small SCHIP-style programs with Kennedy would do the trick. Others ended up tinkering with health-care reform ideas that ended up looking a lot like Obamacare.

In photographs of Governor Romney signing the Massachusetts universal health-care law in 2006, Ted Kennedy stands grinning behind him with Boston's backslapping Beacon Hill Democratic leadership. Those pictures tell the story of Republican fecklessness on health-care reform from the 1990s to present day.

OBAMACARE HAS ALREADY BEEN TRIED— AND FAILED

The most recent Republican failure on health-care reform came during the 2012 presidential election. The GOP candidates pledged to "repeal and replace" Obamacare—though they had more to say about the "repeal" part of that formula than about "replace"—but none of them pointed to real-world examples that showed how the law would eventually fail. The idea of setting up exchanges, relying on Medicaid, requiring individuals to buy government-approved health insurance plans, and then subsidizing their purchase has already been tried. The results have been higher premiums, runaway costs, crowded emergency rooms, and longer wait times.

But Republicans couldn't run against this prototype of failure because it was Massachusetts's "Romneycare," and the man responsible for it was now their nominee for president.

Team Obama's reliance on Romneycare was nothing new. After Scott Brown won a special senatorial election in Massachusetts on an anti-Obamacare platform, the political strategist David Axelrod appeared on ABC's *This Week* to spin the embarrassing news to the Democrats' advantage. "Senator Brown comes from a state that has a health care plan that's similar to the one we're trying to enact here," Axelrod said. "We're just trying to give the rest of America the same opportunities that the people of Massachusetts have."

Lindsey Graham, a Republican senator from South Carolina who appeared on the Sunday talk show after Axelrod, could barely contain himself. "The American people are getting tired of this crap," Graham spluttered. "No way in the world is what they did in Massachusetts like what we're about to do in Washington."[11]

The Massachusetts state treasurer, Tim Cahill, a Democrat, would beg to differ. He pointed out the conceptual and architectural similarities between the two plans: "If President Obama and the Democrats repeat the mistake of the health insurance reform adopted here in Massachusetts on a national level, they will threaten to wipe out the American economy within four years."

By 2010, the commonwealth's Medicaid costs had risen from $7.5 billion to an estimated $9.2 billion under Romneycare. According to an analysis released by Cahill, more people had coverage, but only 32 percent of the 407,000 newly insured paid for their insurance entirely on their own. The remaining 68 percent were partially or wholly subsidized by the taxpayers. Only 5 percent of the newly insured Massachusetts residents who were not receiving any state benefits obtained their coverage through the state's "Connector" health-care exchange. In 2010, only 23 percent of those enrolled in Massachusetts's state-managed health insurance programs paid anything toward their coverage. About 99,000 newly insured residents now received free coverage through Medicaid. Another 87,000 received 100-percent taxpayer subsidies through the Connector's "Commonwealth Care" program. Furthermore, another 26,000 were legal immigrants ineligible for federal subsidies who benefitted under the Commonwealth Care Bridge program.

Cahill argued that Romneycare was manageable because the federal government could bail out the program, especially through Medicaid. "Who, exactly, is going to bail out the federal government if this plan goes national?" he asked.[12] It was a good question. Romneycare defenders pointed out that the Massachusetts law still polled well statewide and that Cahill was getting ready to run an (ultimately unsuccessful) independent campaign for the governorship, giving him an incentive to take shots at the bipartisan consensus of the Bay State. Nevertheless, it didn't bode well for Obamacare.

The *Boston Globe* reported in 2008 that the wait to see doctors in Massachusetts had grown to as long as a hundred days. Kaiser Health News noted, "A survey conducted by the Massachusetts Medical Society found patients can wait as a long as a month and a half for non-urgent physicians' appointments."[13] Emergency room visits rose by 9 percent between 2004 and 2008.

The theory behind both Romneycare and Obamacare was that the uninsured were major drivers of emergency room crowding. It turns out that Medicaid patients use emergency rooms disproportionately, so expanding Medicaid coverage is unlikely to ease the strain. Nationally, 97 percent of emergency room doctors told the American College of Emergency Physicians that they treated patients "daily" who were covered by Medicaid but couldn't find primary care doctors who would take them. "The results are significant," said ACEP's president, Sandra Schneider, on National Public Radio. "They confirm what we are witnessing in Massachusetts—that visits to emergency rooms are going to increase across the country, despite the advent of health care reform, and that health insurance coverage does not guarantee access to medical care."[14]

So increasing access won't necessarily bring down costs, as we have been told. It would have been nice to have that conversation during the presidential campaign.

OBAMACARE IS ONLY THE BEGINNING

The inevitable failure of Obamacare to control costs is one of the reasons Paul Krugman feared Democrats had miscalculated by abandoning the public option. He warned them back in 2009:

> Imagine that reform passes, but that premiums shoot up (or even keep rising at the rates of the past decade.) Then you could all too easily have many people blaming Obama et al. for forcing them into this increasingly unaffordable system. A trigger might fix this—but the funny thing about such triggers is that they almost never get pulled.[15]

Krugman probably needn't worry. The *Washington Examiner*'s Philip Klein outlines a more plausible scenario:

> At some point in the future, liberals will be arguing that any ongoing problems with the health care system are a

result of Democrats leaving the private sector with too much control. They'll be renewing their push for a "public option," with the ultimate goal of achieving single-payer health care. And if Republicans don't present compelling alternatives, that's exactly where America will end up.[16]

Big government is the only institution that is touted as the solution to its own failures. If there is a major national security breach because some government agency didn't do its job, the immediate response is to give the agency more power. It's as if, at the height of the Enron scandals, people concluded that the problem was that Ken Lay didn't have enough authority.

From a conservative perspective, the upside to Obamacare is that it is easier to repeal or substantially rework than single-payer health care. But it is something liberals can build on as well. It is not a permanent substitute for single-payer. Obamacare is just the first of many steps along the way to greater federal control of the health-care sector. Republicans, conservatives, and libertarians had better grasp the meaning of these developments before it's too late.

THE HEALTH OF THE STATE

Health care has been a major driver of government spending and debt. The increasing costs of medical care have also made millions of Americans more tolerant of—and reliant upon—big government.

The economist Gary Becker and Judge Richard Posner report that there was a nearly 80-percent increase in premiums for employer-provided health insurance from 2000 to 2009. "Much of this is nominally paid by the employer," they write, "but because it is a cost of labor it substitutes for wage increases and so holds wages down."

For millions of Americans, wages are no longer rising with productivity. According to one estimate, the inflation-adjusted median household income fell 4 percent between 1997 and 2008. Middle-class wage stagnation has made many voters more susceptible to liberal economic arguments. Policies designed to limit or shrink government in many cases don't speak to their financial circumstances or anxieties. For many of these people, in fact, health-care costs gobble up more of their take-home pay than taxes. Even some businesses that have traditionally been disinclined to support government health-care programs may now find it financially appealing to have a public option cover their employees instead.

When it comes to solving problems in health care, whether they stem from cost or access, expanding government is often the path of least resistance. It is the obvious way to cover the uninsured. Before Obamacare, we often heard that the United States was the only major industrialized nation without a nationalized health-care system. It is certain that we will continue to hear that the private sector plays a larger role in the U.S. health-care system than in those of our major competitors. But the United States does not have a genuine free market in health care. Instead it has a patchwork of private and public coverage, with the former in many cases having a parasitic relationship with the latter. The tax code still discriminates against people who want to purchase health insurance for themselves rather than rely on their employers. Myriad regulations stifle choice and competition. Yet government is still the first place people tend to look for solutions to the problems in health care.

Opponents of government health care often deny that the problems with America's health-care system before Obamacare were as serious as reformers claim. They point out that the number of uninsured was often exaggerated, that the quality of care was high, and that most people were satisfied with the care that they received, at least according to some major polls. Nevertheless, the number of voluntarily uninsured Americans stretched into the millions. Rising health-care costs are a major source of worry for struggling families. Even if Barack Obama had never been president, rising costs were driving major government growth through increased Medicare and Medicaid spending.

Conservatives, libertarians, and Republicans, who have seemed unaware of these facts and thus out of touch with reality, have unwittingly made big government seem like the only solution.

From food to housing, most other basic human needs are provided by the free market with a government safety net. Most people do not starve or become homeless as a result. Only a small fringe suggests that universal government provision of these goods is necessary for them to be widely enjoyed. Yet conservatives have too often been uninterested in applying the lessons of the free market to our health-care problems. Republicans have contented themselves with playing defense and hoped to beat the Democrats, when they weren't copying them.

Surely we can do better. If we don't, big government is here to stay.

CHAPTER EIGHT

LESSONS IN SHRINKING GOVERNMENT

B ig government is an unstoppable force. That's the most com-
mon objection faced when one talks about cutting spending
or rolling back regulations. Sometimes even conservatives
make this argument.

Consider a *Wall Street Journal* op-ed by Peter Berkowitz that
announced in the subtitle, "Big government and the social revolution are here to stay."[1] Berkowitz is a senior fellow at the conservative Hoover Institution and author of *Constitutional Conservatism:
Liberty, Self-Government, and Political Moderation.* Apparently where
constitutional conservatism and political moderation conflict, moderation should win. "Conservatives can and should focus on restraining spending, reducing regulation, reforming the tax code, and
generally reining in our sprawling federal government," Berkowitz

advised. "But conservatives should retire misleading talk of small government. Instead, they should think and speak in terms of limited government."

"It is important for Republicans to recognize that the battle is over," wrote Charles Krauthammer in the *Washington Post*. The estimable conservative columnist concluded, "Years ago, Republicans suicidally carried on against the New Deal long after it had been accepted by most citizens as part of the fabric of American political life."[2]

Some conservatives even welcome the changes government growth has wrought. Blogging at *U.S. News & World Report*, Scott Galupo worried that the constitutional challenges to Obamacare would blossom into a full-blown challenge to postwar big government. "But a well-educated faction of conservatives see it as a vessel for larger ambitions: It's a chance for the court to restore the proper constitutional understanding of untrammeled economic liberty," Galupo fretted. "To put it mildly, such ambitions scare the crap out of me."[3]

We have arrived at a point where preserving government at a size that will necessitate perennial trillion-dollar deficits, staggering tax increases, rampant inflation, or some combination of the three, is less scary to many Americans than restoring constitutional boundaries.

There are objections to the case for conservative acquiescence to big government. Berkowitz's vision of limited government is impossible without large cuts to the welfare state—or at least gradual reforms that will result in less spending over time. If we're talking about government limited by the Constitution, there is no way to square a three-trillion-dollar federal budget with Washington's real enumerated powers. Similarly, Berkowitz's policy objectives of "restraining spending, reducing regulation, reforming the tax code, and generally reining in our sprawling federal government" are all unattainable so long as government continues to assume so many powers and functions.

Krauthammer's column mentioned the conservative campaign against big government only in passing. It was actually written in 1992 about the alleged end of the "abortion wars." Krauthammer began by asserting, "The abortion debate is over." Pro-lifers, he concluded, had lost. "One can reasonably declare a great national debate over when all three independently elected branches of government come to the same position," Krauthammer argued. The Supreme Court, then without "a single Democratic appointment in 25 years," had just reaffirmed *Roe v. Wade*. Bill Clinton, a "down-the-line pro-choice president" who "pledged to appoint abortion-rights judges," had just been elected, alongside pro-choice Democratic majorities in both houses of Congress.[4]

Yet twenty years after Krauthammer wrote these words, abortion remained a hotly debated topic. The number of abortions, the abortion rate, and popular support for the pro-choice position all subsequently fell. A Gallup poll in May 2012 found that the percentage of Americans identifying as "pro-choice" was at an all-time low. Self-described pro-lifers outnumbered pro-choicers by 50 percent to 41 percent. Three years earlier, Gallup even found a slim pro-life national majority.

That's not to say that the abortion debate was completely transformed. Abortion is still restricted only at the margins. Pro-choice candidates, while failing to enact sweeping measures like a federal law guaranteeing the right to abortion, still win some important elections. *Roe* remains substantially intact after forty years. But the debate over abortion is clearly not over, and opponents have made progress that the conventional wisdom—plus the three branches of the federal government—once considered impossible. Even opinion leaders do not always know where public opinion or political conditions will go. This is especially true when a dedicated group of activists continues to fight, undaunted by long odds and willing to speak the truth.

RENT SEEKING AND RATCHET EFFECTS

Nevertheless, there are good reasons to argue that big government is what Russell Kirk might call a "permanent thing." Cutting government is extremely difficult and rarely accomplished. In a perversion of Say's Law ("supply creates its own demand"), the supply of government creates its own demand. In an essay in *National Review* in 2005 on the "smallness and weakness of the constituency for limited government," Ramesh Ponnuru wrote, "There are more voters who care deeply about keeping the Small Business Administration in operation than there are voters who care deeply about shutting it down."[5] The breakneck growth of a deficit-financed welfare state makes it inevitable that more voters will develop similar attachments to proliferating government programs, though the broad-based tax increases that they entail will dampen the enthusiasm of some.

The economist Robert Higgs described the "ratchet effect" in his landmark book *Crisis and the Leviathan*. A war or some other crisis causes government to grow, leading to the assertion of new powers or the creation of additional bureaucracies. When the crisis passes, the tide of state power recedes but not to its pre-crisis levels. Thus with each emergency, the size and scope of government grows a bit more, and much of that growth is permanent. The financial crisis of 2008 is a textbook example of this phenomenon. Obama's former chief of staff, Rahm Emmanuel, encouraged his fellow liberals to "never let a crisis go to waste."

The historical record is discouraging. According to the Office of Management and Budget, year-over-year government expenditures, adjusted for inflation, have fallen only four times since 1980: 1987, 1993, 2007, and 2010. And on closer examination, it's even worse—spending barely changed in 2007, and the federal government failed to pass a budget in 2010.

"So why exactly would anyone expect Congress to really cut spending down the road if it has shown essentially no ability to rein in spending in the near term?" asks Nick Gillespie, the editor of *Reason* magazine. "This is like a variation on the old joke about losing money on every unit sold but making it up in volume. Except it's not like that at all. Or funny."[6]

WHEN SPENDING WAS CUT

The president and Congress have occasionally tried to cut spending. Since World War II, Republicans have launched a frontal assault on federal spending exactly three times: the "do-nothing Congress" of 1947–48, the Congress that came in with Ronald Reagan in 1981–82, and the Newt Gingrich Congress of 1995–96. Each attempt was different from the others, and each carries lessons for future government-cutters.

Although Harry Truman found it an effective election-year jibe, "do-nothing Congress" presented itself as a misnomer. With the first Republican majority since 1933, it was arguably the most successful postwar conservative Congress. Led by Senator Robert Taft, the Rand Paul of his day, the Eightieth Congress rolled back the militarization of the U.S. economy and prevented the creation of a full-blown European-style welfare state. This Congress cut spending across the board. With Hitler defeated and Pearl Harbor avenged, there were steep cuts in military expenditures. Federal spending had reached its wartime high of 43.6 percent of GDP as recently as 1944. Taft's troops pared it down to 11.3 percent in 1948. Wartime price controls on food and other consumer products were repealed. Taxes were cut. The peacetime draft was, at least temporarily, suspended. The Taft-Hartley amendments to the Wagner Act passed over Truman's veto and checked the power of big labor, which enjoyed a symbiotic relationship with big government.

After World War II, liberals had hoped to grow the federal government even beyond its New Deal size. The Eightieth Congress quashed those hopes. Eleanor Roosevelt promoted government-sponsored daycare, but the Republicans shut her experiments down. Truman proposed a national health-insurance program modeled after the British National Health Service. His plans were rejected. Even when government grew, it grew by less than progressives had hoped. After the war, there was an expanded federal role in the housing market. But the Do-Nothings largely confined this role to financing. Bureaucrats wouldn't end up building and managing vast housing projects—for the middle class, at least.

Some of these bad ideas took decades to return. Others never emerged again. Truman's health-care plan was more government-run than even Obamacare. Taft-Hartley helped prevent organized labor from playing as dominant a role in American politics as it played in much of Western Europe. "For liberals, the postwar years represented the best—perhaps the only—opportunity for the construction of a European-style social democracy in the United States," observed the journalist David Frum. "Thanks to Taft and his Republicans, that opportunity was lost."[7]

THE REAGAN REVOLUTION

After the spending cuts of the Eisenhower era, there was no concerted effort to limit—much less to shrink—the federal government until after the 1980 presidential election. The Reagan landslide swept in a Republican-controlled Senate. Republicans also increased their ranks in the House and along with a group of mostly Southern Democrats called the Boll Weevils were able to form a conservative working majority.

Not since Barry Goldwater had the Republicans nominated a presidential candidate with such a strong rhetorical commitment to limited government. Not since Calvin Coolidge had such a candidate actually been elected to the White House. "In this present crisis, government is not the solution to our problem," Reagan proclaimed in his first inaugural address. "Government is the problem." He went on to ask, "Well, if no one among us is capable of governing himself, then who among us has the capacity to govern someone else?"

In 1981, the American people were tired of high taxes and rampant inflation. But after years of the New Deal and the Great Society, they had become inured to a big-spending government. Reagan had campaigned on a platform of boosting defense expenditures while cutting social programs, policies that would redirect the federal budget to constitutional purposes. Once in office, Reagan's spending priorities were attacked by labor unions, civil rights groups, feminists, unionized teachers, and environmental activists. No Republican administration since Eisenhower had taken on so many liberal sacred cows. Every activist group on the left found something to hate in Reagan's agenda.

Lane Kirkland, the president of the AFL-CIO, accused Reagan of practicing "occult economic experiments on the American people" (apparently a play on George Bush's line about "voodoo

economics"). Kirkland said Reagan's budget "helps the wealthy at
the expense of middle-class workers and the poor, comforts the
comfortable, and afflicts the afflicted." If the Left did not mobilize
against Reagan, Kirkland warned, "The administration's program
will produce human suffering in the short run and retard economic
growth enough to haunt us for years to come." He added, "It is ironic
that conservatives who so long ranted against liberal experiments
in social engineering should now be willing to turn our society into
a vast laboratory for academic theorists of the likes of Laffer and
Friedman."[8]

The NAACP joined the attack, calling his program an attempt to
"appease middle-class taxpayers whose attention to the billion dollar defense budget is diverted by the apocryphal 'welfare queen.'" In
a speech to the civil rights group, Reagan countered that "government is no longer the strong draft horse of minority progress."
Economic freedom was, the president insisted.

Teachers' unions forecast an educational apocalypse. "The Reagan revolution," cried Robert Gruenberg, a spokesman for the
National Education Association, "means the beginning of the break-
down of public education. It means a 25-to-40-percent cut in revenues in some localities. Over 200,000 public school employees could
lose their jobs." Feminists detected sex discrimination, noting that
most families on welfare were headed by single women. "This year's
budget fight is the most severe challenge we've ever faced," fretted
Janyce Katz of the National Women's Political Caucus.

In April 1981, the *Christian Science Monitor* published an article
about the various groups gearing up to oppose Reagan: "Special-
interest lobbies prepare to defend their 'turf,'" The *Monitor* reported,
"Lobby groups under attack are showing a greater sophistication
and inventiveness in their responses to the Reagan revolution
here.... The result promises to be more bite and clarity in the

months ahead in national debate" from the groups that "will likely bear the burden of Reagan spending, tax, and regulatory reforms."[9] Maybe not clarity, but certainly bite.

Congressional Democrats were not much more restrained. Ted Weiss of New York summed up Reagan's budget as "Drop dead, America!" Fellow New Yorker Thomas Downey predicted it would "kill people." Michigan's John Conyers labeled it "an economic crime."[10]

Aside from his own immense political talent, which few advocates of government-cutting have come close to replicating, Reagan had two things going for him. First, a large number of conservative Democrats in the House represented districts that Reagan had carried by a wide margin. That helped him counter the heavy hand of the liberal speaker of the House, Tip O'Neill, a legendary Massachusetts Democrat.

One of the leaders of the Boll Weevils was Phil Gramm, a former economics professor serving as a Democratic congressman from Texas. Gramm exhorted the House's conservative Democrats, torn between an inclination to vote for Reagan's budget cuts and a fear of O'Neill's reprisals, to "draw the line in the sand." If William Barrett Travis had asked for a debate at the Alamo instead of drawing a line in the sand, Gramm told them, "there never would have been a battle." When his fellow Texas Democrat Jack Hightower mordantly noted that everyone who crossed the line at the Alamo had died, Gramm conceded the point, but retorted, "the ones who didn't cross the line died, too. Only no one remembers their names."[11]

Reagan's second advantage was almost a national tragedy. On March 30, 1981, as the president was leaving the Washington Hilton, he was shot by John Hinckley. One of the bullets lodged less than an inch from Reagan's heart.

"I hope you're all Republicans," Reagan joked with the doctors as he was wheeled into surgery. He later told his wife, "Honey, I forgot to duck." Such grace literally under fire resonated with the American people. The president not only survived an assassination attempt at age seventy, but he also laughed in the face of danger.

At that point, even Tip O'Neill knew the battle was lost. "I've been in politics a long time, and I know when to fight and when not to fight," he told reporters the night before Reagan returned to give a speech to Congress. By May, the president's job approval rating stood at 67 percent.

The legislative conquest that ensued was impressive. The top marginal income tax rate was slashed from 70 percent to 50 percent. A three-year tax cut reduced rates by 25 percent across the board. There was a business tax cut, and income taxes were indexed to inflation, halting the unlegislated tax increases of "bracket creep." Domestic discretionary spending was cut by 14.2 percent in Reagan's first year. There was a 32-percent reduction in spending for mass transit. The inflation-adjusted federal education budget fell by 17.7 percent over four years. All told, the early round of spending cuts totaled some $64 billion.

The conventional wisdom is that Reagan may have cut social programs, but his tax cuts and defense spending increases blew a hole in the budget. Tax revenues, however, continued to rise. Even though Reagan subsequently agreed to tax increases, his tax cuts were much larger and marginal rates continued to fall. An initial drop in receipts was the result of the 1982 recession and the Federal Reserve's tight-money policy under Paul Volker. If federal spending had grown no faster than inflation between 1979 and 1989, there would have been a budget surplus despite the Reagan tax cuts and defense buildup. Even with more rapid spending growth, the deficit had fallen to 2.9 percent of GDP by the last year Reagan was in office.

In his book *The Struggle to Limit Government*, John Samples of the Cato Institute concludes that Reagan did not succeed in shrinking government but did limit its growth. "Many programs were sharply restrained in the first two years of Reagan's presidency," writes Samples, noting that the tax cuts were substantially larger than the budget cuts. "After the 1982 recession, Reagan had less sway over Congress and thus less power to cut spending."[12]

Nevertheless, discretionary spending—including defense but not entitlements—remained essentially unchanged, adjusting for inflation, from 1981 to 1989. In fact, it was $27 billion lower when Reagan left office than when he came in. As the economy grew, sparked by tax cuts, federal spending dropped to 21 percent of GDP.

REVOLUTION 2.0

The third Republican attempt to cut federal spending came with the Gingrich Congress, elected in the 1994 midterm elections. The star of that show was indisputably the new Speaker of the House, Newt Gingrich, with impressive supporting performances by his lieutenants Dick Armey (the policy wonk) and Tom DeLay (the tactician). Much of the heavy lifting, however, came from John Kasich, chairman of the House Budget Committee, and Bob Livingston, chairman of the House Appropriations Committee. In addition, they were encouraged by a zealous conservative freshman class ready to keep them honest.

Kasich came up with a budget plan that would eliminate nearly three hundred programs, including the Corporation for Public Broadcasting (bye-bye, Big Bird), the Travel and Tourism Administration, the Advanced Technology Program, and the International Trade Administration. Many of these programs had been on the chopping block early in the Reagan administration. But Kasich was even more aggressive in his desire to shut down cabinet-level agencies. While Reagan had wanted to close the Departments of Education and Energy, Kasich threw in the corporate-welfare headquarters of Commerce, too. The ambitious Budget Committee chairman also wanted to balance the budget in seven years, by 2002.

Kasich knew he would face serious opposition. "It will be very difficult, because of the 'Zorro Principle'—death by one thousand cuts," Kasich told the reporter Elizabeth Drew. "People affected by a government program will be very vocal that the program be maintained—they'll organize in members' districts and say why that member must vote to continue the program."[13] His job was harder because so many of the programs he wanted to eliminate had supporters within the Republican caucus. Even the National Endowment for the Arts, whose notorious funding decisions had attracted ferocious criticism, was no sure bet for abolition.

Most ambitiously, the House Republicans sought to reduce the rate of growth of Medicare. In 1995, the program was already on shaky financial ground, and reforms were needed to keep it from bankrupting the country. But Republicans would soon be reminded why even Reagan was afraid to touch entitlements.

First, the size of the projected Medicare savings ($270 billion) was so close to the estimated size of the Republicans' proposed tax cut ($245 billion) that Democrats could easily accuse them of cutting Medicare in order to pay for tax cuts—"for the wealthy," of course.

Second, Gingrich carelessly talked about letting a particular feature of Medicare "wither on the vine"—a comment that was widely interpreted as hostile to that program's continuation. Democrats used the comment in ads depicting the Republican reforms as a "Trojan horse" for abolishing Medicare altogether.

In politics, if you're explaining, you're losing. Nevertheless, it is worth revisiting exactly what Gingrich said. In a speech to a Blue Cross Blue Shield conference in October 1995, he argued:

> Now let me talk a little bit about Medicare. Let me start at the vision level so you understand how radically different we are and why it's so hard for the press corps to cover us.
>
> Medicare is the 1964 Blue Cross plan codified into law by Lyndon B. Johnson, and it is about what you'd—I mean, if you all went out in the marketplace tomorrow morning and said, "Hi, I've got a 1964 Blue Cross plan," I'll let you decide how competitive you'd be. But I don't think very.
>
> So what we're trying to do, first of all, is say, OK, here is a government monopoly plan. We're designing a free-market plan. Now, they're very different models. You know, we tell Boris Yeltsin, "Get rid of centralized command bureaucracies. Go to the marketplace."
>
> OK, what do you think the Health Care Financing Administration is? It's a centralized command bureaucracy. It's everything we're telling Boris Yeltsin to get rid of. Now, we don't get rid of it in round one because we don't think that that's politically smart, and we don't think that's the right way to go through a transition. But we believe it's going to wither on the vine because we think people are voluntarily going to leave it—voluntarily.[14]

Gingrich was predicting that Medicare would "wither on the vine" because senior citizens would voluntarily leave it for a *better alternative*—not because he opposed health care for seniors. These nuances were immediately lost when the AFL-CIO mounted an expensive ad campaign against vulnerable Republicans based on the Medicare comments.

We have already discussed the government shutdown, which shifted the balance of power away from the Gingrich Republicans back toward the Democrats in the White House. But what was the overall record of this Congress in cutting spending?

The non-defense discretionary budget was cut by 4 percent, the first reduction in such spending since the Reagan administration. Welfare was reformed, ending an entitlement. By 1997, Congressional Republicans reached a budget agreement with the Clinton administration that cut taxes—dropping the capital gains tax rate all the way down to 20 percent—and, with the help of the Internet boom, produced the first balanced budget since 1969. The Freedom to Farm Act set agriculture subsidies on a glide path to elimination.

On the negative side of the ledger, Republicans fell short of most of their goals. The 1997 deal with Clinton increased discretionary spending $29 billion over the caps promised in the 1994 Contract with America. No Cabinet departments were shut down. As the conservative columnist George Will observed, "More than 300 programs have been eliminated, but these were mostly wee things, and the annual savings of about $3 billion about equals the increase since 1995 in the budget (now more than $34 billion) of the Education Department, which Republicans vowed to abolish."[15] The Commerce Department was also 40 percent larger. By 1998, Republican commitment to fiscal discipline was waning. They jacked up farm subsidies in violation of the Freedom to Farm Act. The number of earmarks was exploding.

The revolution was over, almost as quickly as it began.

WHITHER SPENDING CUTS?

Three times America stood on the precipice of social democracy. Three times, largely Republican congresses yanked America back from the brink. And three times the GOP seriously sought to cut spending—twice with a hostile White House. Nevertheless, the results were mixed. What might future government-cutters learn from this political history?

"The 1981–82 Congress contented itself with trimming, limiting, and containing existing programs," observed David Frum. He noted that only two large federal programs—revenue sharing and the Comprehensive Employment and Training Act—were actually abolished. The latter was replaced by a new training program co-sponsored by the future vice president Dan Quayle. "The 1947–48 Congress, though it left much of the New Deal alone, struck decisively when it moved at all," Frum continued. "Price controls were not lifted gradually; they were abolished outright. The closed shop was not tampered with; it was prohibited."[16]

The 1995–96 Congress more closely resembled the 1981–82 edition than the "do-nothing Congress." As a result, many of its achievements were gradually reversed. Farm subsidies were restored; domestic discretionary spending was increased; the surpluses turned back into deficits; and eventually, under Obama, the work requirements for welfare were weakened.

The same fate befell the reforms of the Reagan Congress. Inflation-adjusted non-defense discretionary spending fell 9.7 percent in Reagan's first term and rose 0.2 percent in his second. During the 1990s, domestic spending increased while the defense budget declined with the end of the Cold War.

The Reagan tax cuts proved more durable. But even here there was backsliding. The capital gains tax was raised to 28 percent as part of the 1986 tax reform deal. The business tax cut was nullified. Payroll taxes began rising, eating away at the Reagan tax cuts for the middle class. The top marginal income tax rate jumped in 1990 and in 1993, never returning to its pre-Clinton levels after the Bush tax cuts. Obama is threatening to raise them again.

Frum cites federal housing programs to illustrate the erosion of reform:

> The U.S. spent about $5 billion in housing programs in 1983. The government spent less in 1984 than it had in 1983, less in 1985 than 1984, less in 1986 than in 1985, less in 1987 than in 1986. Then, suddenly, all the gains evaporated: Between 1987 and 1988, housing spending nearly sextupled, to $14 billion. By 1990, the federal government was spending more than $25 billion on housing programs.[17]

Government programs are like weeds. If they are merely trimmed, they will grow back. They must be uprooted when possible.

But another lesson is that big government can be curtailed, even when it is not reversed. Not achieving all of your policy objectives doesn't mean you haven't accomplished anything important.

Success must also be measured by something more ambitious than prevailing at the ballot box. Of the three reforming Congresses we've looked at, the one that was least successful at getting itself reelected scored the most enduring victories against big government. Republicans controlled the Senate for six years under Reagan and the House for twelve years after Gingrich led them to victory in 1994. But they put a smaller dent in big government than the "do-nothing" Republicans of 1947–48, who lost their majority in 1948.

By the time the Democrats retook the House in 2006, the congressional GOP was their partner in big government.

It would be foolish to claim that stopping big government is easy. Many people clearly benefit from government. Others perceive benefits where they may not exist. Most of all, asking politicians to think of something more important than fundraising or reelection cuts against human nature.

But big government has been challenged before, with some success. With some courage—and more than a little luck—it can happen again. Learning from the recent past is a great place to start.

CHAPTER NINE

TEA PARTY TRIUMPH— AND TEMPORARY DEFEAT

What about the Tea Party Congress elected in 2010, the latest group of Republican legislators who came to Washington with the intention of cutting federal spending? How did they fare? Perhaps it is best to ask Representative Thomas Massie, who was sent to Congress in a special election while those Republicans were still freshmen.

"We have been here for two years," said Massie, a Kentucky entrepreneur with a degree in mechanical engineering from the Massachusetts Institute of Technology, "and we haven't cut anything."[1] Massie knows something about cutting spending. When he was judge-executive of Lewis County in northern Kentucky—a position akin to a county commissioner—he received a telephone call from the county jailer. The facility's hot water heater needed to be replaced at an estimated cost of twelve thousand dollars. That was too much money, Massie decided. He went online and ordered a hot water heater on eBay for $5,500 with free shipping and a warranty. He then had it shipped to the jail, where he installed it himself with the help of three inmates.

Massie took his first college-level macroeconomics course from Paul Krugman, the liberal Nobel Prize–winning economist who now writes for the *New York Times*. "It didn't make sense then, and it doesn't make sense now, [Krugman's] version of it," he joked to *Roll Call*. The congressman understands the value of a dollar.[2]

The same can't be said for all of his colleagues, Republican or Democrat, which is why Massie's assessment of the 112th Congress is unfortunately true. Divided government—bipartisan power-sharing—has tapped the brakes on spending growth but hasn't come close to rolling back the gains big government made from 2009 to 2011.

ONE THIRD OF WASHINGTON

Republicans have had their biggest majority in the House since the do-nothing Congress, but they have much less to show for it. In fairness, John Boehner's House faced much longer odds. Not only did they face a hostile president in Barack Obama—as did their postwar predecessors—but the Democrats continued to control the Senate.

Every successful conservative Congress in the modern era benefited from a Republican-controlled Senate. The Speaker of the House, John Boehner, and the Tea Party freshmen not only had to contend with Obama, but also they couldn't get their preferred legislation out of Harry Reid's Senate.

In fact, it could be argued that Reid's Senate made the 112th truly a do-nothing Congress. Despite a federal law requiring it to do so, this Congress failed to pass a budget. Reid is as responsible as any leader in Washington for the federal government being funded entirely through stopgap measures for nearly four years; so much for Republican obstructionism.

Without a Democratic Senate majority, the president would have had much less leverage in dealing with congressional Republicans. There was no guarantee that the Democrats would keep the upper chamber in the elections of 2010 and 2012: Democrats had to defend nineteen seats to the Republicans' eighteen in 2010, and an eye-popping twenty-three seats to the Republicans' ten in 2012.

Poor candidate recruitment is one commonly cited reason that the Republicans did not retake the Senate, and thereby improve their bargaining posture, either time. But another reason is that after the passage of the unpopular health-care bill, Senate Democrats were never again asked to cast votes for controversial legislation. The Democrats did not push for "comprehensive immigration reform." The cap-and-trade bill that passed the House, which would have increased taxes on energy consumers, was never taken up in the Senate. The Democrats failed to advance a budget precisely because it would put their members on record as supporting gargantuan spending, difficult cuts, or future tax hikes. To govern is to choose, says the old cliché. But sometimes to hold power is to choose not to govern. After the Tea Party elections of 2010, Republicans learned that it's impossible to govern the country from the House alone.

LEMON PLEDGE TO AMERICA

That's not to say that the House Republicans always put their best foot forward. They came in with big goals in 2010. To their credit, they laid out a vision for reducing spending and controlling the debt-to-GDP ratio while the Democrats largely evaded this

responsibility. They voted on more than one occasion to repeal, if
not replace, Obamacare. But the House Republicans stopped well
short of supplying a serious challenge to the growth of government
during Obama's first two years in office. The party was divided on
how to proceed and how aggressively to pursue conservative policies.

When it looked like Republicans might take both houses of Congress in 2010, there were calls for more ambitious reforms. The
House Republicans looked back to their Contract with America from
1994 and decided to follow up with a new Pledge to America. It has
long been debated how important the Contract with America really
was in winning the GOP majorities of '94. Even some conservatives
now look back on the Contract as a Washington gimmick. But the
platform was generally popular. Gingrich had asked the pollster
Frank Luntz to test each item, and he included only issues with at
least 60-percent support. The Contract gave the party a concrete
legislative agenda.

The Contract's actual results were mixed. House Republicans
fulfilled their promise to bring all ten items to the floor for a vote at
least, although not all of them passed. Some of the bills that cleared
the House were bottled up in the Senate, despite a Republican
majority. But when the party moved beyond the Contract, it lost
direction.

After 1996, when both Bill Clinton and the Republican congressional majorities were reelected, Paul Gigot of the *Wall Street Journal* called the new House GOP plan a "Contract with Ambivalence."
Back then, Joe Scarborough wasn't an MSNBC host but a conservative congressman from Florida who was disenchanted with his
party's listlessness.

"Quite a few members are obviously concerned over the direction that the leadership has taken in these first three months,"
Scarborough complained at the time. "We have a concern that our

leadership remains shell-shocked from the government shutdown a year and a half ago. Most of us are ready for them to start leading again rather than sitting back and reading from Clinton's song sheet."[3]

That was the Newt Gingrich-led Congress, two years in. The leadership of the Republican majority that took over the House after the 2010 elections seemed like it was *still* shell-shocked. Many of its veterans had helped swell federal spending under George W. Bush.

One promise in the less-memorable Pledge to America was $100 billion in spending cuts—a modest figure given the trillion dollars in annual deficits. In the age of Obama, spending $100 billion was the work of an afternoon. But $100 billion in cuts seemed achievable. Based on the experience of John Kasich and Bob Livingston in the 1990s, it was an amount that could be wrung from the appropriations process—which the Republicans were going to control—and might be expected to survive negotiations with Obama, who was sure to oppose most cuts in non-defense spending.

In February, however, just one month after the new majority was sworn in, the House Appropriations Committee prepared a continuing resolution that would have cut $58 billion from the president's languishing proposal for a 2011 budget. The freshmen and some conservative backbenchers protested. They had run on cuts of a full $100 billion. Calm down, the leadership replied. The $58 billion was actually consistent with the promise to cut $100 billion, they argued, because the fiscal year was nearly half over. To the leadership, this was a reasonable way to achieve savings in a dysfunctional budgetary process. To the freshmen, it sounded an awful lot like what George W. Bush might call "fuzzy math."

House Republicans ultimately passed $61 billion in cuts, but this time the Democrats balked. They would agree to only about $30 billion. If they could not come to an agreement on how to fund federal operations for the next six months, Boehner's young majority already faced the prospect of a government shutdown. For liberals, the situation seemed almost too perfect. The very confrontation that saved Clinton's bacon in the '90s would save Obama's now. This gave the Democrats little incentive to compromise.

Todd Rokita, a freshman Republican congressman from Indiana, told me at the time that the memories of the 1995–96 shutdown were "seared into the minds" of his longer-serving colleagues. But he didn't feel that way. "In 1995, I was more interested in chasing girls than in what Newt Gingrich was doing," the forty-one-year-old Rokita joked.

"The people who seem to be afraid of a government shutdown… are worried about getting elected in two more years," Texas Republican Blake Farenthold told the *Washington Post*. "I'm worried about having to go home and tell the folks that I grew up with, and intend to spend the rest of my life with, that I'm a liar."

Yet the freshman class as a whole was not so antagonistic toward the speaker or the rest of the leadership. They reserved their fire for the other side of the aisle or for Harry Reid in the other chamber. A group of thirty House freshmen sent Reid a letter. "Mr. Reid, your record on spending in the Senate is one of failure," they wrote. "We do not accept your failure as our own."

Republicans were still unified for the most part. "We may have different strategies for getting there," said South Dakota Representative Kristi Noem, "but we are united in our desire to cut spending." Lou Barletta, who had been the mayor of Hazelton, Pennsylvania, before winning his first House term in 2010, used a football analogy instead: "Some of us want to throw a Hail Mary right into the end zone and others want to take a few plays to get there, but we all have the same goal."[4]

What about repeatedly spiking the ball to stop the clock?

HONEY, I SHRUNK THE DEFICIT REDUCTION

The Democrats played hardball as the first government shutdown in fifteen years loomed. "Republicans want to shut down our nation's government because they want to make it harder to get cancer screenings," Harry Reid said with characteristic restraint. "They want to throw women under the bus."[5]

Mainstream media reports were only slightly less alarmist. Here's how the Associated Press described the evils that were to follow:

> A closure would mean the furloughs of hundreds of thousands of workers and the services they provide, from processing many tax refunds to approving business loans. Medical research would be disrupted, national parks would close and most travel visa and passport services would stop, among many others.[6]

Democrats also sought to divide the GOP's leadership from the party's conservative base. "The Republican leadership has the Tea Party screaming so loudly in its right ear that it can't hear what the vast majority of the country demands," Reid continued. "I remain confident that if we're serious about getting something done, we should be able to complete a deal and get it passed and avert a shutdown," Obama told reporters. Then in Pennsylvania, he made an amazing statement, given the Senate Democrats' record. "At a time when you are struggling to pay your bills and meet your responsibilities, the least we can do [is] meet our responsibilities to produce a budget," Obama told an audience. At that time, the Democratic-controlled Senate hadn't passed a budget in nearly two years.

Republicans were under a great deal of pressure to resolve the impasse without breaking faith with their voters. "Republicans have no interest in shutting down the government," Boehner asserted. But "we are going to fight for as many spending cuts as we can get."[7] By this point, the Senate had already rejected the Republicans' $61 billion in spending cuts. The three previous temporary spending measures had contained some $12 billion in cuts. With serious budget reductions effectively off the table, the two parties were separated by only about seven billion dollars for the remainder of the fiscal year.

Democrats insisted that they had met Republicans more than halfway, while GOP leaders knew they had come far down from their opening bid of $100 billion in cuts. Republicans had tried to fund the Pentagon for the rest of the year, defund Planned Parenthood, and cut another twelve billion dollars in spending, but the Senate ruled that a nonstarter. Time was running out.

At the eleventh hour, a deal was reached. It was advertised as including $38 billion in cuts. The *Washington Post* reported, "The cuts, if enacted, would add up to the largest budget reduction for federal agencies in U.S. history," calling it a "sign of [conservatives'] power." "Inside a few months," the *Post* story continued, "an ascendant Republican Party has managed to impose its small-government agenda on a town still largely controlled by Democrats." The *New York Times* quoted Boehner as calling the package the "largest real-dollar spending cut in American history."[8]

Fiscal conservatives saw things differently. It wasn't as if a national debt ballooning its way to $16 trillion could be dealt with through savings in half a fiscal year, to say nothing of the unfunded liabilities of the country's major entitlement programs. But the $38 billion didn't bode well for Congress' ability to do big things. The chairman of the Republican Study Committee, Jim Jordan, complained, "voters are asking us to set our sights higher."[9]

It soon became clear that even the $38 billion in cuts were illusory. According to the Congressional Budget Office, the actual deficit reduction for fiscal year 2011 was just $352 million in the context of a $1.5 trillion shortfall. *Politico* reported:

> Congressional Budget Office data, posted Wednesday morning, shows that total non-emergency appropriations will fall to $1.0498 trillion, a nearly $38 billion reduction from their level at the beginning of this year. But the impact on outlays or direct spending before the 2011 fiscal year ends Sept. 30 will be just $352 million compared to prior CBO reports....[10]

Throw in contingency funds for Afghanistan and Pakistan, and suddenly discretionary spending for fiscal year 2011 was $3.3 billion *higher*, not lower, than the CBO estimated in December 2010.

Republican leaders pushed back angrily, emphasizing that non-emergency appropriations had been contained at $1.0498 trillion, the advertised $38 billion less than at the beginning of the year. Boehner's office issued a statement explaining the difference between outlays and budget authority, accusing reporters of buying into "Democratic spin": "The final agreement cuts nearly $40 billion in budget authority—taking away the Administration's license to spend that money—which will result in deficit savings of $315 billion over the next decade."[11]

Given the magnitude of the problem, some felt that the $352 million in net savings or even forty billion dollars in budget authority was missing the point. "Even $38 billion out of the $3.8 trillion is just not enough," said Representative Justin Amash of Michigan, one of the fifty-nine Republicans who voted against the deal. "I'd prefer that the leadership not describe cuts like these as historic or substantial."[12]

"Our debt here is going to double in the next ten years," said Senator Marco Rubio of Florida. "We have to start solving it now. We can't wait any longer. We're running out of time. And this deal just doesn't do it. In fact, it's full of a bunch of typical Washington, D.C., gimmicks. I'm just not going to be a part of that."[13] Many House freshmen voted for the compromise, however, including Rokita and Farenthold.

DANCING ON THE CEILING

By the summer of 2011, Obama was again at odds with the Congressional Republicans, this time over the national debt ceiling. The country had almost borrowed its way to the statutory limit and was bumping up against an August 2 deadline. This time, the GOP wanted assurances that the borrowing was under control before agreeing to a nearly $2.5 trillion increase in the $14.3 trillion debt ceiling.

Some proposed that the hike in the debt limit be accompanied by a balanced-budget amendment to the Constitution. But a constitutional amendment would require two-thirds majorities in both houses of Congress, plus ratification by three-fourths of the states. It was unlikely that Republicans would have anything to show for such a deal.

Another idea was to tie a higher debt limit to cuts in federal spending, perhaps even entitlement reform. Most Democrats, however, would not even discuss such a proposal. They argued that when Republican presidents like Ronald Reagan and George W. Bush needed the debt ceiling raised, it simply happened. In a speech on the Senate floor, Reid noted that Congress had raised the debt limit seventy-four times since 1962 without any concessions.

Obama himself said, "The American people are not interested in the reality TV aspects of who said what and did somebody's feelings get hurt." It was time to raise the debt ceiling. "These are obligations that the United States has taken on in the past," he insisted. "Congress has run up the credit card, and we now have an obligation to pay our bills."[14]

Many Republicans wanted to match the debt ceiling increase dollar-for-dollar with spending cuts. "Using Congressional Budget Office data, I have calculated that if we apply this every time we reach the debt limit over the next 10 years, we will balance the budget by 2021 without raising tax rates over current rates," wrote Ohio Senator Rob Portman, a former Republican White House budget director. "That's more than $5 trillion in spending cuts over the decade."[15]

The president argued that a debt fix should be easy, but complained, "members of Congress are dug in ideologically." He called for a "balanced plan" that included some revenue from tax increases on those in the higher brackets. "I have not seen a credible plan— having gone through the numbers—that would allow you to get to $2.4 trillion without really hurting ordinary folks," Obama said. "And the notion that we would be doing that, and not asking anything from the wealthiest among us or from closing corporate loopholes—that doesn't seem like a serious plan to me."[16]

This time around, conservatives united around a single proposal. The "Cut, Cap, and Balance" plan sprang from a framework designed by the conservative Republican Study Committee in the House. The idea was to make discretionary and mandatory spending reductions that would cut the deficit in half in a year; to impose enforceable, statutory budget caps designed to bring federal spending in line with the 18 percent of GDP consumed by revenues; and to send the states a strong balanced-budget amendment that also limited spending.

Cut, Cap, and Balance enjoyed the support of the leading conservatives in Congress: Jim DeMint, Pat Toomey, Ron and Rand
Paul, Jim Jordan, even old bull Orrin Hatch, who was then about to
face a primary challenge for his Senate seat. Several GOP presidential candidates also signed a pledge in favor of the proposal. "There's
an old country song that says if you don't stand for something, you'll
fall for anything," DeMint said as it was rolled out.[17] More importantly, the proposal attracted the support of conservatives outside
of Congress and electoral politics.

Needless to say, the plan went nowhere among Democrats—or
the media. "Cut, cap, and balance pledge complicates debt-ceiling
calculus," blared a *Washington Post* headline. "Even if it fails,"
sniped CNN's Candy Crowley, "it has endless potential as a CBS—
campaign bumper sticker."[18] How droll. Crowley's network trotted
out "fiscal experts" who said that the plan would cut spending too
quickly (a novel problem in Washington), contained the wrong mix
of vagueness and detail, and was just a distraction anyway since the
Senate was unlikely to pass the plan. The most valid criticism was
that GDP wasn't defined consistently, which was important for how
the spending caps were to be set.

The reality of Obama's spending in 2009 and 2010 was that any
attempt to restore the pre-Obama fiscal status quo was going to
require large cuts. With big numbers comes sticker shock and political backlash.

Soon there emerged discrepancies between the Cut, Cap, and
Balance pledge and the congressional plan. The pledge language
committed signers only to embrace the framework of offsetting debt
ceiling increases with "substantial" spending cuts, a balanced-budget
amendment that also eschewed tax hikes, and imposing spending
caps. It was not a pledge to back the bill that was in play in the House.

A version of Cut, Cap, and Balance passed the House anyway, though only after losing the support of Michele Bachmann and Ron Paul for not cutting enough up front. "I have never voted to raise the federal debt limit, and I have no doubt that we face financial collapse and ruin if we continue to grow our debt," Paul said in a statement. "We need to make major spending cuts now, in this budget, and we can no longer afford to allow more deficit spending based on promises of future cuts."

Nine Republicans defected, but five Democrats voted with the Republicans. That was more than enough to make Cut, Cap, and Balance more bipartisan than Obamacare. But the plan was declared dead on arrival in the Senate. "We don't have any more time to engage in symbolic gestures. We don't have any more time to posture," Obama said. Reid called the balanced-budget amendment "the stupidest constitutional amendment I've ever seen," despite his previous support for a different version of the idea.

"The president continues to say that he wants to do big things. We do as well. We put forward our big plan and vision in our budget," House Majority Leader Eric Cantor countered. "But we implore the president—let's do big things, let's go ahead and get our fiscal house in order. But let's do so without imposing higher taxes on the small business people that we need so desperately to start hiring again."[19]

SUPER BAD

By August, the president and Senate Democrats were once again at loggerheads with House Republicans. This time the consequences—default—were potentially much worse than any government shutdown. The government, after all, could be reopened with relatively few lingering aftershocks. But on the first of the month, the familiar pattern reemerged. Just as with the government shutdown and the first expiration of the Bush tax cuts at the end of 2010, the two parties were able to find a resolution only at the last minute.

In exchange for an increase in the debt ceiling, the deal purported to contain $2.1 trillion in deficit reduction over the next ten years. An immediate cap was imposed on domestic spending, requiring $917 billion in cuts in a decade. The law created a bipartisan debt-reduction task force—the so-called "super committee"—that was responsible for coming up with recommended spending cuts that were guaranteed an up-or-down vote by Congress. If the super committee, composed of an equal number of Democrats and Republicans from both houses, came up with $1.2 trillion to $1.5 trillion in cuts, the debt ceiling would rise by a commensurate amount.

Erskine Bowles, the Democratic co-chairman of the president's fiscal commission (and who therefore knows something about how these panels fail), tried to play good soldier, calling the deal "a good first step." But Bowles also admitted to *USA Today*, "It's not a whole loaf. It's not half a loaf. It's a couple of slices."[20]

If the super committee failed, it would trigger at least $1.2 trillion in automatic spending cuts, to be taken equally from defense and non-defense discretionary spending, a process known as sequestration. The prospect of draconian cuts was supposed to create incentives for success rather than failure: Democrats wouldn't want $600 billion in domestic spending cuts, and Republicans would prefer to avoid cutting the military by that much (or opening the door to tax increases). Sequestration would kick in at the same time the temporary extensions of the Bush tax cuts were scheduled to expire, creating a Keynesian nightmare of simultaneous tax hikes and spending cuts. Surely the political class couldn't fail under these circumstances, could it?

Yes, it could. The super committee failed spectacularly. The result was the threat of one of the biggest self-inflicted wounds in American political history, the "fiscal cliff." Washington's habit of delay in dealing with its fiscal problems was becoming extremely dangerous, even in the short run.

The debt-ceiling deal wasn't even enough to avert a downgrade of the United States' credit rating. On August 5, 2011, for the first time in history, Standard & Poor's denied the U.S. government an AAA rating, just four days after the compromise was announced. The debt-ceiling deal didn't even amount to Erskine Bowles's few slices of bread. This was a trail of crumbs that America's political leaders were incapable of following home.

FROM NANNY STATE TO NATIONAL SECURITY STATE

Don't let it be said that Democrats and Republicans can't come together when they truly want to. Toward the end of 2012, as the fiscal cliff loomed, with our budgetary challenges conspicuously unmet, the two parties united—to increase government power.

The first issue at hand was the National Defense Authorization Act for fiscal year 2013, which funds much of our defense spending. Since late 2011, it has also contained a provision that many experts on the left and the right interpret as allowing for the indefinite detention without trial of American citizens. Section 1021 was intended for suspected terrorists, of course, rather than ordinary criminal defendants. But it gives a great deal of discretion to the government to determine who should be held without charges or trial—discretion the Founding Fathers arguably did not intend to give when drafting the Constitution and Bill of Rights, particularly the Sixth Amendment.

The ACLU's executive director warns that this "statute is particularly dangerous because it has no temporal or geographic limitations, and can be used by this and future presidents to militarily detain people captured far from any battlefield." In the war on terror, the battlefield is undefined and there is no clear end to hostilities. Senator Lindsey Graham, in fact, clarified that the American homeland was part of the battlefield in his statement of support for the controversial provision. "When they say, 'I want my lawyer,' you tell them: 'Shut up. You don't get a lawyer,'" Graham thundered on the Senate floor. "You are an enemy combatant, and we are going to talk to you about why you joined Al Qaeda."[21]

That is certainly a fitting way to talk to a terrorist. But what if the American in custody is innocent? Are we to believe that the federal government is incapable of running a health-care exchange but is infallible concerning homeland security?

When the provision for indefinite detention was originally added to the NDAA, Obama signaled that he might veto the bill, but only because it didn't give the president *enough* discretion over detention. The White House later withdrew its veto threat. "We have concluded that the language does not challenge or constrain the president's ability to collect intelligence, incapacitate dangerous terrorists, and protect the American people," read its statement.

The legislation nevertheless passed both houses of Congress easily, despite splitting Democrats and attracting forty Republican opponents in the House. But the following year, there was enough concern for the Senate to pass a bipartisan amendment that the California Democrat Dianne Feinstein and the Utah Republican Mike Lee sponsored. The Feinstein-Lee amendment states, "An authorization to use military force, a declaration of war, or any similar authority shall not authorize the detention without charge or trial of a citizen or lawful permanent resident of the United States apprehended in the United States, unless an Act of Congress expressly authorizes such detention."

The Feinstein-Lee amendment failed to satisfy those who thought it suggested that the right to trial is subject to congressional whim, but it passed the Senate sixty-seven to twenty-nine. Rand Paul, the Tea Party Republican senator from Kentucky, hailed the amendment's passage as a "HUGE win for the Constitution, the Bill of Rights, and an 800-year precedent" (emphasis his). But Feinstein-Lee did not survive the conference committee that resolved the differences between the House and Senate versions of the NDAA. John McCain chaired that committee.

"The relevant section, entitled 'Rights Unaffected,' preserves not just the right to habeas corpus, but all constitutional rights enjoyed by every person before a court of the United States," McCain's communications director protested. "To suggest that the chairman and ranking members of the congressional defense authorization committees somehow stripped those rights is just wrong."[22]

Senator Paul switched from a "yes" vote to a "no" vote on the NDAA as a result. "These core American legal privileges prescribed in our Bill of Rights have been observed since our nation's founding," he explained. "When I assumed office, I took an oath to protect our Constitution—and in voting against this unconstitutional NDAA, I kept that promise." But the rest of the Senate voted eighty-one to fourteen in favor of the NDAA without the amendment they had passed the previous month. The majority included Dianne Feinstein herself. The House passed the act 315 to 107.

Next up was the federal government's warrantless surveillance program. A deeply polarizing policy when Bush was president, like so much else it met with little opposition with Obama in the White House. Hardly anyone objects to the government's having the tools to listen to communications between those who would do Americans harm. But the data collection methods lend themselves to intercepting much more than that. How much more? Nobody knows. Even members of Congress who have asked have not gotten direct answers. And most of them don't want to know.

Rand Paul argued that just by looking at credit card statements, "the government may be able to ascertain what magazines you read, whether you drink and how much, whether you gamble and how much, whether you're a conservative, a liberal, a libertarian, whom do you contribute to, who is your preferred political party, whether you attend a church, a synagogue or a mosque, whether you see a psychiatrist, what type of medication do you take."

"By poring over your Visa statement, the government can pry into every aspect of your personal life," the senator continued. "Do you really want to allow your government unfettered access to sift through millions and millions of records without first obtaining a judicial warrant?"

The warrantless wiretapping program is under the authority of the Foreign Intelligence Surveillance Act, part of a package of amendments originally adopted in 2008 that "sunset" or expire every five years. When they were set to expire in early 2013, senators from Oregon asked two questions: How does the secret FISA court actually interpret the law? And how does it affect the privacy of the American people as a whole, as opposed to the type of people we would like to be spying on? It is understandable that the FISA court would operate in secret, given the sensitive nature of the surveillance involved. But keeping the precedents secret is like trying to interpret the Constitution with a highly classified Supreme Court. What we're left with is guesses.

The Senate voted against learning about what the FISA court was up to by fifty-four to thirty-seven and said "no" to assessing the privacy impact by fifty-two to forty-three. (Both amendments specifically made allowances for keeping information vital to national security secret.) Only a dozen senators voted to apply Fourth Amendment protections to text messages and emails. At the height of the Obamacare debate, Nancy Pelosi infamously said we needed to pass the bill to see what was in it. FISA is already law, and we still can't learn what's in it.

Despite railing against these surveillance powers as a presidential candidate, Obama has stepped up domestic wiretapping as president. Relying on Justice Department records, the ACLU announced a "huge increase in warrantless electronic surveillance" from 2009 to 2011. Obama quickly and privately signed into law the renewal of provisions he once promised to overhaul. The headline of an article by David K. Shipler in *Salon* put it well: "Liberals let Obama get away with unconstitutional actions."[23] As do the rest of us.

There is no bipartisan consensus or plan of action for getting our nation's fiscal house in order. But the two parties can still come together to devour freedom.

WHAT WENT WRONG?

From Scott Brown's special election victory in Massachusetts in early 2010 to the Republicans' recapture of the House of Representatives, the Tea Party had high hopes. Aside from tax-cut extensions, those hopes have been largely dashed. The country is on a course set to double the national debt in ten years. Congressional Republicans, from the most "establishment" to the most Tea Party, have done little to alter that troubling trajectory. How did this happen?

To some extent, opponents of big government underestimated how hard it would be to change the country's path from the House alone. They also overestimated the degree to which the American people understand the details of the federal budget and what's at stake. On the positive side, more people now grasp that the federal government is spending money it doesn't have. At some point, that is going to lead to greater demands on average taxpayers, whether in higher taxes or a lower standard of living as the Federal Reserve debases the currency. One way or another, budgets of three to four trillion dollars and deficits of one to two trillion dollars will have consequences.

Elections also have consequences. The country elected and reelected Barack Obama. Americans elected and reelected a Democratic Senate. Conservatives who believe they can govern as if they have unified control of the federal government are guaranteed to be disappointed.

The electorate may not have understood that a vote for Obama and Reid is a vote for bigger government, more debt, and insolvent entitlement programs. They may not have understood that the higher taxes will inevitably hit not just "millionaires and billionaires"—if they can ever be so confined—but all of us. They may not have realized what Obamacare would mean for their freedom. But that's how they voted, and the best that House Republicans—and their counterparts in the Senate—can do is to try to contain the damage. If they care to, that is.

In Chapter Three, we learned that many Republicans are no more interested in cutting spending and enforcing the Constitution than the majority of Democrats. Some of these big-government Republicans are in the leadership. Others would like to get spending under control, but are fearful of the political consequences. They know smaller government is often more popular in the abstract than in practice.

With the advent of Fox News, talk radio, and the conservative blogosphere, it is easy to forget what we discussed in Chapter Four:

the power of the mainstream media. Efforts to shrink government often come across badly. It's easy to depict budget-cutters as snatching food from the mouths of hungry children. Journalists who approach the private sector with skepticism often extend a generous benefit of the doubt to the public sector.

Despite these headwinds, there really is no excuse for conservatives' propensity to make the responsible look irresponsible and to make sound management of the country's finances look reckless. After all, Ronald Reagan faced media more hostile than Newt Gingrich or Mitch McConnell have faced. He campaigned in a more homogenously liberal media environment than Mitt Romney or Todd Akin. Yet Reagan was much more successful than any of the Republicans I've just named.

So is it time to give up? Surrender is not necessary—and not even an option. As Trotsky supposedly said of war, you may not be interested in government, but government is interested in you.

Even the failures of big government's foes offer important lessons. For the first time in history, when Republicans make decisions about government spending, they are under pressure to cut and then cut more. The GOP is facing pressure from its right now, not just its left. Some of the Republican confusion stems from not knowing how to deal with this new reality; they are discombobulated.

It would have been better if conservative pressure groups were so aggressive and so effective when Republicans actually held power. Some, like the Club for Growth, were still coming into their own when George W. Bush was in power. Others, like Heritage Action and Young Americans for Liberty, didn't really exist.

Sometimes they may expect too much from outgunned House Republicans in the short term. But it is good that they are aiming high and finally taking politics as seriously as their liberal counterparts do. The same coalition that supported George McGovern in a landslide defeat supports Obama through two terms today; the left didn't give up.

The solution isn't to stop fighting. It's to fight smarter and better.

The voters may not be asking us, but the country needs us to set our sights higher.

CHAPTER TEN

A TIME FOR FIGHTING

Barack Obama had not yet been sworn in as president for the second time when the next budgetary crisis hit. This one, like big government itself, was entirely manufactured by the political class. "Look with favor on our nation and save us from self-inflicted wounds," prayed the Senate chaplain.[1]

The prayer was offered up too late. The so-called fiscal cliff was really a perfect storm of political failure and indecision. The super committee created to come up with spending cuts as a condition of the debt ceiling deal, predictably, failed. After all, it was the inability of Congress to agree on budget priorities that led to the creation of the committee—a typical Washington blue-ribbon commission—in the first place.

But to give members a sense of urgency and some incentives for both parties to reach an agreement, the debt ceiling law also included sequestration: a series of across-the-board spending cuts that would be imposed automatically if the super committee was unable to come up with the required savings on its own. The sequester would take effect at the same time that the Bush tax cuts, which Obama and another lame-duck Congress temporarily renewed at the end of 2010, expired.

So if Congress didn't act, there would be a combination of tax hikes and budget cuts. It was a Keynesian's worst nightmare, especially at a time of chronic unemployment and anemic economic growth. Nevertheless, there was some suspicion that Obama wanted to go over the cliff's edge. It made more sense than any of the deficit-reduction proposals contained in his own swollen budgets, and it would give him additional revenues to fund government growth while blaming Republicans for the result.

What could go wrong?

THE SHALLOW CLIFF

While a universal tax increase would indeed have been economically counterproductive, not to mention burdensome to the cash-strapped American people, the spending cuts forced by sequestration were actually trivial. Most of them were "cuts" only in the Washington sense—namely, plans to increase spending by less than the baseline. The economist Robert Murphy calculated that, if we had gone over the cliff, the supposed $487 billion in deficit reduction in the first year would actually come out to $478 billion in tax increases plus a paltry $9 billion in spending cuts.[2]

This is apparently what the president means by a "balanced approach" to deficit reduction—one that is 98.2 percent increased taxes and 1.8 percent spending cuts. The cuts would have amounted to three-tenths of 1 percent of federal spending, and expenditures still would have risen the next year. Compared to the baseline, however, the savings would number in the hundreds of billions.

"When the economy fails to revive," predicted the historian Thomas E. Woods, "this will be blamed on the alleged 'austerity' program of the federal government, without noting that the laughable 'spending cuts' were vastly exceeded by the tax increases."[3] This is true of many claims that European austerity programs have been economically calamitous—more of the austerity came from growth-killing tax hikes than from spending cuts that would allow resources to remain in the productive private sector.

There were different ways of crunching the numbers to yield slightly different conclusions, and some economists who rely upon different baselines and economic assumptions argued that the spending cuts would have been larger than Murphy estimated. But by any measure, the tax increases and spending cuts were grossly imbalanced, and the spending cuts weren't as large as many supposed.

Most members of Congress, however, did not want sequestration to take place. The administration said it didn't either. "No one wants it to happen," White House senior adviser David Plouffe told reporters. "No one thinks it should happen."[4] Obama, during his final debate with Mitt Romney, flatly predicted that it wouldn't happen.[5] "First of all, the sequester is not something that I've proposed," Obama insisted misleadingly. "It is something that Congress has proposed." The president signed the debt ceiling deal, which created both the super committee and the sequester.

Sequestration is a somewhat arbitrary way to cut government spending, and it is a particularly cavalier way to treat the federal government's legitimate constitutional functions, such as national defense. But it is not without defenders. While Congress got out from under sequesters mandated by the Gramm-Rudman-Hollings

Deficit Control Act of 1985, it cut spending more than it would have otherwise. "Gramm-Rudman worked," Phil Gramm, the Texas senator who was a primary sponsor of the law, argued in the foreword of an economics book. "Between 1985 and 1990, it cut the deficit by 40 percent and the size of government relative to the economy by 10 percent."[6] Gramm liked to cite these figures during his unsuccessful 1996 campaign for the Republican presidential nomination.

Senator Rand Paul thought Congress should go through with sequestration. In a summer 2012 meeting with a small group of reporters on Capitol Hill, he needled colleagues who, unlike him, voted for the deal that called for the sequester in the first place, but now wanted to stop it from happening. "They all vote to raise the debt ceiling with a military sequester, and now they're all caterwauling about it," Paul said, noting that he voted against the bill. But he thought if anything was going to get cut, sequestration might be necessary—even for the Pentagon budget. "I'm of the belief that nothing around here will ever be efficient unless the top-line number is lower," Paul continued. "To me, [sequestration] means that the top-line number is lower, and if you really believe in savings in the military budget *or else you'd have to find the savings*, you'd be forced to find the savings."[7]

In other words, if there are specific spending cuts and caps, politicians will have to wring out the inefficiencies they always claim are in the federal budget but never cut. If they can't cut the fat, they risk meat and bone.

Some conservatives—particularly activists who didn't need to seek reelection—were willing to go over the cliff. "I want conservatives to stay strong," Christine Morabito, president of the Greater Boston Tea Party, told a newspaper. "Sometimes things have to get a lot worse before they get better."[8]

KICK THE CAN

In the end, that was the path that neither the Obama administration nor Congress chose. Republicans were divided. They didn't want taxes to go up on anyone, but they didn't want to be blamed in the media for an across-the-board tax increase. The worst-case scenario was the Bush tax cuts for the middle class lapsing and then returning as the Obama tax cuts, after a taxpayer revolt with the GOP accused of holding taxpayers hostage to protect the rich.

The need to avert a tax hike complicated conservative efforts to gain meaningful concessions on spending. It was clear that the same gridlock that led to the super committee's creation, and then to its failure, was going to prevent real cuts from passing. In addition to Obama's reelection, Democrats gained seats in the Senate and, with some justice, blamed their House minority on Republican-led redistricting rather than a popular reprimand.

House Speaker John Boehner had reportedly hoped to reach a "grand bargain" with the White House, combining sweeping tax and entitlement reforms, but the sides were too far apart. Boehner could not get the president to budge enough on spending to sell anything to his own caucus. Obama kept pressing for tax revenues.

In private meetings and thinly veiled public comments, Obama made clear he was going to use the bully pulpit against Republicans if the fiscal cliff talks failed. "Mr. Obama repeatedly lost patience with the speaker as negotiations faltered," the *Wall Street Journal* reported. "In an Oval Office meeting last week, he told Mr. Boehner that if the sides didn't reach agreement, he would use his inaugural address and his State of the Union speech to tell the country the Republicans were at fault."

"I put $800 billion [in revenue] on the table," Boehner reportedly said at one point. "What do I get for that?"

"Nothing," the president shot back. "I get that for free."[9]

For Republicans and conservatives, there were no good options. The final bill, a product of negotiations between Vice President Joe Biden and Senate Minority Leader Mitch McConnell, was unpalatable.

On the positive side, more than 80 percent of the hated Bush tax cuts survived. The top Clinton tax rate of 39.6 percent was reinstated only for individuals earning at least $400,000 annually and families with yearly incomes in excess of $450,000, both White House concessions. There were some minor savings against the budget baseline. But neither the sequester nor any other serious spending cuts were included.

Some of the figures that disappointed activists floated in the hours after the fiscal cliff deal, such as the 41 to 1 ratio of tax increases to spending cuts, were exaggerated. But the reality was bad enough: according to the Congressional Budget Office, the pact added nearly $4 trillion to the deficit over ten years.

In fiscal year 2013, the deficit was projected to increase $330 billion for a shortfall of $971 billion—a mid-sized federal program away from $1 trillion. The additional revenues from the income tax rate increase on the "wealthy," if they ever materialize, may not even offset the tax benefits for green energy.

Although income tax rates did not rise as much as they could have, the expiration of the payroll tax holiday meant a regressive tax increase on 77 percent of the American people. Obama's team encouraged people to utilize social networking sites to talk about how they would spend the $2,000 the president would supposedly save them by preventing middle-class tax increases. How surprised and disappointed they were to find the money missing from their paychecks anyway.

With the phase-out of deductions, the real top marginal rate for some taxpayers will climb to 41 percent. Factor in the Obamacare surtax on investment income, which comes out to 3.8 percent; and Medicare, slated at 0.9 percent; and some will be faced with a 46 percent rate. The legislation was called the American Taxpayer Relief Act, naturally.

While it could have been much worse, it was still the largest tax increase in nearly twenty years in exchange for no real concessions on spending, no deficit reduction, and no plan to bring the debt-to-GDP ratio to a sustainable level. Erskine Bowles, the former chief of staff to Bill Clinton, and Alan Simpson, the former Republican senator from Wyoming, co-chaired the president's fiscal commission. Neither of them was impressed with the deal, calling it a "real missed opportunity." While Simpson and Bowles perceived the debt ceiling and fiscal cliff legislation as necessary first steps, "neither one nor the combination of the two come close to solving our Nation's debt and deficit problems." They added, "Washington missed this magic moment to do something big to reduce the deficit, reform our tax code, and fix our entitlement programs."[10] "This thing isn't going to do anything, really," Simpson said later on *Meet the Press*. "What the hell? Who's kidding who?"[11]

It's become a tired cliché in Washington to talk about "kicking the can" down the road. But no other metaphor better describes the federal government's aversion to getting its fiscal house in order.

CHAMPAGNE WISHES, PLATINUM DREAMS

If anything, the establishment's thinking on this subject has grown even more frivolous as time has passed. It's almost as if the new normal has inured them to any sense of the government's limits—even math.

As a second debt ceiling showdown loomed in early 2013, one popular idea making the rounds was that the Treasury should mint a one–trillion-dollar platinum coin. You read that correctly. Mint collectible platinum coins and deposit this newly created "wealth" at the Fed in order to continue paying the federal government's bill if the borrowing limit hasn't been raised. This isn't a fringe phenomenon. Paul Krugman has expressed support for the proposal. Even center-right pundits have been covering it favorably in their opinion columns. The discussion has dominated the political and economic blogosphere.

Perhaps the only value the coin concept has created was Megan McArdle's response in the *Daily Beast*. "Never mind that the law was never intended for this, and that these sort of hypertechnical legislative games might trigger the very political and financial crises they are supposed to avert," she wrote. "Seemingly, the most important thing is for the president to defeat intransigent Republicans—even if that means that the president 'for all Americans' who once spoke of winning the future and healing the planet will be reduced to presiding over the Franklin Mint." McArdle continued, "The Great Platinum Coin Caper is everything that is wrong with Washington: a stupid partisan maneuver that erodes the institutions of our government for no gain other than an immediate political win."[12]

Another argument circulating is that the president should simply invoke the Fourteenth Amendment and raise the debt ceiling unilaterally. Obama initially rejected this as unworkable. "I have talked to my lawyers," he said. "They are not persuaded this is a winning argument."[13]

The Fourteenth Amendment states, "The validity of the public debt of the United States, authorized by law, including debts incurred for payments of pensions and bounties for services in suppressing insurrection or rebellion, shall not be questioned." The historical context was making sure Union debts were repaid at the conclusion of the Civil War, while repudiating Confederate debt. But that hasn't stopped overly literal-minded politicians—who wouldn't normally think of themselves as strict constructionists—from attempting to apply it to contemporary problems.

One congressman even came up with a Civil War analogy in order to defend the approach. Representative Danny K. Davis, an Illinois Democrat, likened it to the Emancipation Proclamation, which had just marked its 150th anniversary. "Sometimes when we've gotten great answers is when presidents have had enough authority to take some actions," he said.[14] Nothing says "emancipation" like enslaving future generations to debt.

Less radically, some in Washington say the fiscal cliff pact paves the way for future tax increases. Before the ink on the deal was even dry, the Obama administration was so outspoken in this belief that some speculated the White House was trying to persuade congressional Republicans to vote against it. "Keep in mind that just last month Republicans in Congress said they would never agree to raise taxes on the wealthiest Americans," Obama said. "Obviously the agreement that's currently being discussed would raise those rates and raise them permanently."[15]

A White House source boasted to Fox News, "Obama broke [the] tax pledge," one of the "most consequential policy achievements of the last couple decades." Another "senior official" said future tax increases would be easier to get from Republicans "because they've already crossed that threshold."[16] David Axelrod took to ridiculing anti-tax activist Grover Norquist on Twitter.

Jonathan Cohn, writing in the *New Republic*, argued that the American people were still not paying as much in taxes as they had in the past, and that the complaints should stop. "Nobody likes paying taxes, but everybody likes the services that taxes finance," he concluded. "The Republican strategy is to make people focus on the former and ignore the latter."

All of these reactions convey an air of denial about the government's spending and debt. Boehner claims the president told him, "We don't have a spending problem." Democratic senator Dick Durbin of Illinois made the startling, arithmetically challenged claim, "Social Security does not add one penny to our debt—not a penny."[17] Durbin uttered this fantastical fallacy in the context of saying he was open to entitlement reform—but didn't want to really touch Social Security or Medicare, the two largest entitlement programs. White House spokesman Jay Carney backed him up, saying, "Social Security currently is not a driver of the deficit." In the long term, that's just not true. In fact, Social Security started running a cash-flow deficit in 2010, exacerbated but not exclusively caused by the now-expired payroll tax holiday.

Congressional Republicans haven't looked much better. Shortly after the November 2012 elections, they purged four strong fiscal conservatives—Justin Amash of Michigan, Tim Huelskamp of Kansas, David Schweikert of Arizona, and Walter Jones of North Carolina—from their preferred committee assignments. Amash and Huelskamp were kicked off the House Budget Committee. The House leadership allegedly kept secret scorecards concerning these rogue Republicans. Among their crimes? They supported balancing the budget within a five-year window, as the balanced-budget amendment most congressional Republicans supported would do.

RED INK REBELLION

Amidst this bad news, however, there are some good things to report. At every stage of the budget battles, conservatives fought longer and harder than ever before to prevent excessive spending and borrowing. While liberals mock it as "hostage-taking," the very idea of attaching conditions to debt ceiling extension is not only new—it is overdue.

When the Republican congressional leadership first signaled it was willing to give ground on taxes and spending, conservative groups outside Congress and backbenchers in the House balked. Groups like the Club for Growth, FreedomWorks, and Heritage Action said they would hold members accountable for fiscally irresponsible votes. The pressure was no longer coming exclusively from those who wanted to spend more money the government doesn't have.

When Boehner proposed his "Plan B" in the fiscal cliff negotiations shortly before Christmas 2012, conservative activists were outraged. Not only had they not been briefed on the details, but Republicans were also abandoning their opposition to tax increases without any deal on spending. These activists said no dice—and so, surprisingly, did a critical mass of House Republicans.

The House adjourned for the holidays without taking up Boehner's plan. Moderate Republicans were irate. Outgoing Ohio representative Steve LaTourette defended Boehner and blamed the "same forty, fifty chuckleheads" that "have screwed this place up" all year. LaTourette has since joined the Main Street Partnership, which he fittingly enough has pledged to make less Republican.

Some protested that the million-dollar threshold for tax increases in Plan B was higher than what Congress ultimately agreed to, so House Republicans miscalculated. This Monday-morning quarterbacking missed one key detail—neither the White House nor the Senate Democrats were willing to accept Plan B, despite favoring most of its details in the past. Republicans would have been giving up on taxes in the opening gambit for nothing.

Despite an 85 to 8 vote in the Senate, House Republicans ended up voting against the final bill by a margin of 151 to 85. It took a majority of Democratic votes to pass it. This time, freshmen members like Todd Rokita and Blake Farenthold, as well as departing long-time congressmen like Roscoe Bartlett, voted against their leadership. They voted no.

The fiscal cliff deal even briefly endangered Boehner's speaker-ship. As the 113th Congress convened, a disorganized band of GOP rebels plotted a coup. They did not agree on a single challenger. They did not settle on a specific strategy, other than that of denying Boehner a first-ballot victory. They did not even have a reliable whip count of who was with them.

One of their informal ringleaders wasn't even going to serve in the new Congress, outgoing representative Jeff Landry of Louisiana. Their social media campaign, intended to fire up the conservative base, was run by a twenty-three-year-old activist with fewer than two thousand followers on Twitter. Matthew Boyle of Breitbart News was one of the few reporters to take them seriously.

The plot predictably failed, prompting media scorn. But what only a few reporters noticed was that anti-Boehner votes briefly spiked to seventeen—the exact number necessary to force a second ballot, at which point anything was possible. Only last-minute defec-tions saved him from having to face another round of voting.

Despite a Keystone Cops-like organization, wavering support, and some unrealistic predictions made by supporters, the effort came surprisingly close. "If I knew what was going to unfold, I would have hung around for a few more days," Landry later said. "To me, that's what's amazing. If we had done a little more, John Boehner would be packing his bags."[18]

Whatever your views on Boehner's speakership, the event revealed the power that opponents of big government had even in the minority—if only they could learn how to use such power wisely.

BIG GOVERNMENT VS. MATH

This is the point in the book where you might expect to find some policy recommendations for dealing with big government. Today Washington teeters on the precipice of bankruptcy. The American people have a government that spies on them, erodes their Bill of Rights protections almost across the board, taxes them, regulates their lifestyle choices, threatens their freedom regarding firearms, and still can't pay its bills.

But some of the policy recommendations are obvious. What remains less obvious is the strategy. Conservatives, as I have said, have a knack for making the fiscally responsible seem irresponsible. In fighting concerted efforts to grow big government and consolidate its past gains, we tend to shoot from the hip. In standoffs between congressional Republicans and the White House, a pattern has developed. Republicans speak as if they are going to stand firm, leverage or no leverage, raising the ire of liberals who oppose spending cuts and moderates who oppose perceived obstructionism and just want everyone to get along. Then at the last minute, the GOP caves in, angering conservatives. Everyone is upset with the Republicans and the government keeps getting bigger.

Changing that dynamic won't be easy. The Republican leadership doesn't appear to be particularly interested in cutting government, at least not when it entails political risk. The party doesn't have the power to implement the kinds of reforms that will keep entitlements solvent, prevent the economy from being consumed by debt, and hold the line on taxes—even if it wanted to do so. The country does not yet seem persuaded that such reforms are even necessary.

The most advanced liberals believe that the deficits are solely the result of the weak economy. Their solution to deficits is to borrow and spend more money, believing that this will ultimately increase revenues and reduce dependence on social programs by growing the economy. Why this preposterous conviction isn't ridiculed as much as is the Laffer Curve, I don't know.

Of course, there is an economic-growth component to the current deficits. But the answer isn't more spending and multiplier effects. The answer is lightening the burden of government on the private sector, so that the real economy can grow. Here even the conventional economic statistics are stacked against the opponents of big government: they measure a dollar spent by Washington without taking into account whence that dollar came.

Government grew when Republicans controlled both the White House and Congress. Divided government, as recently as the Clinton years, has a better record containing federal spending. But that may change. A great deal of government spending now increases automatically. Elected Democrats are moving farther away from the needed reforms.

But at some point, even the gimmickry and triviality of Washington must give way to the harsh reality of math. Our current tax burden will not fund our existing spending commitments. One or the other must give way. Maintaining middle-class entitlements means raising middle-class taxes.

"The first truth is that the current tax rates cannot support the promises made to middle-class Americans," writes Cliff Asness in a magazine published by the American Enterprise Institute. "The most unaffordable items in fiscal projections are Social Security for everyone and government-sponsored health care for the middle class. You cannot preserve these even with Draconian slashing of military, infrastructure, welfare, education, and other expenditures."[19]

A PARTY OF LIMITED GOVERNMENT AT LAST

When Republicans are out of power, they are advised to wait to take on big government until they have prevailed at the ballot box and are safely ensconced in power. Once Republicans are in power, they are advised not to cut spending or they will be bounced from office. There is never a good time to cut spending. The GOP has generally taken this advice. Dwight Eisenhower, Richard Nixon, Gerald Ford, George Bush, and George H. W. Bush all protected or expanded the welfare state, with only Eisenhower and the first Bush even nibbling around the edges. The last two Republican presidents to take on big government, with varying degrees of success, were Ronald Reagan and Calvin Coolidge. And because Reagan only moderated the growth of government, the last Republican president actually to govern in the way the party likes to see itself was Silent Cal.

"Can anyone say the GOP, if it is the party of small government and low taxes, has over the past eighty years been a successful party?" asked the columnist Pat Buchanan. "Or does the America of today look more like the country Socialist Norman Thomas had in mind in 1932?"[20]

But either way, the party must take different advice, and soon. The great political reporter Robert Novak proclaimed, "God put the Republican Party on earth to cut taxes. If they don't do that, they have no useful function." Current spending is making it difficult to cut taxes at all, and impossible to cut them for the middle class. This problem will get worse. A national party cannot win majorities by promising to keep taxes low on a few hedge fund managers.

Some counsel the GOP to get in the business of big government, or to use Mitt Romney's terminology, "giving gifts." That is actually a longstanding Republican tradition. Theodore Roosevelt, after all, was a progressive. But the GOP can't win a bidding war with the Democrats. As Jack Kemp argued, the only thing Republicans have to compete with the left's redistributive cornucopia is the promise of growth. But the days when they can eschew spending cuts as "root-canal politics," to borrow another Kemp phrase, are over. Pro-growth conservatism is off the table once we become pro-growth for government.

In a European-style welfare state, Republicans will take power only in the kinds of circumstances under which Rudy Giuliani became mayor of New York City: completely irresponsible and unresponsive Democratic government. It will be the exception rather than the rule, the fate that has befallen most big-government center-right parties of Europe.

An unwillingness to take short-term political risks—especially at a time when most Republican House members hail from safe districts and most GOP senators are from red states—will inflict long-term, perhaps permanent, pain. The Taft do-nothing Congress may have lost the 1948 election, but its spending cuts kept America from becoming the kind of polity that would never have elected Eisenhower, much less Reagan. Paul Ryan's thankless task of keeping our spending commitments in line with our historical tax burden has become the only path to prosperity for the party as well as the nation.

Republicans who are committed to the fight against big government may have to fight their leaders first. This process may need to begin with the marginalized backbenchers. In the 1990s, Speaker of the House Newt Gingrich lashed out against a group of eleven fiscal conservatives who had opposed him on a budget vote. He demanded that they defend themselves to the entire GOP caucus. "The eleven geniuses who thought they knew more than the rest of the Congress are going to come up and explain their votes," Gingrich said, calling the dissidents "you conservatives."[21] But Steve Largent, an Oklahoma Republican and former wide receiver for the Seattle Seahawks, stood up to Gingrich.

"Mr. Speaker, I am not intimidated," Largent began. "I have been in rooms much smaller than this one when I was on the opposite side of teammates during a players' strike against the NFL. The guys in those rooms weighed 280, 320 pounds and not only *wanted* to kill me, if they had gotten hold of me they probably *could* have. This isn't the case here tonight." Largent denied that he and his ten conservative colleagues had let the team down. He said their team was their constituents, not a group of politicians in Washington, D.C.[22]

Mark Neumann, a Republican congressman from Wisconsin elected in 1994, was kicked off the House Appropriations Committee for voting against leadership. Joe Scarborough, a congressman from Florida who currently hosts the last conservative show on MSNBC, later recalled that Neumann's fellow GOP freshmen, mostly conservatives, sent a letter saying, "Put him back on the committee or we're going to vote against every bill you send up."

"I was quickly reinstated because my freshman colleagues and the conservative movement united and jumped to my defense," Neumann confirmed. "Now is the time for conservatives who are concerned with out of control spending to say to GOP leadership—'enough is enough, we are uniting behind these principled conservative congressmen.'"[23]

In 2007, while Republicans were in the minority, Representative Jeff Flake of Arizona was dismissed from the House Judiciary Committee for "bad behavior." His misbehavior appeared limited to voting against fellow committee members' earmarks—many of them also belonged to the Appropriations Committee—and criticizing the party's overspending on *60 Minutes*.[24] Flake's career, however, wasn't over. He was elected to the U.S. Senate in November 2012, winning an opportunity to vex the leadership in another chamber.

ATTITUDE ADJUSTMENT

These kinds of rebellions need to be encouraged rather than discouraged. There needs to be new thinking as well. Some Republicans believe their fortunes would improve if the party picked fewer fights and if conservative groups such as the Club for Growth backed off. It would have been nice had conservative pressure groups used their considerable influence as effectively when the GOP had more power than they have done since Republicans controlled only the House. Some of these groups, like Heritage Action, are new and didn't exist at the time. Others have felt it necessary to get more involved in primaries.

But it is important to create constituencies for limited government. Republican leaders must also face consequences for growing government, not only for attempts to cut it. As these groups refine their approach, they will reap dividends over the longer term.

The biggest failing of Tea Party organizations hasn't been an excessive commitment to principle: it has been insufficient attention to candidate quality. In fact, conservatives need to keep in mind political philosophy and results rather than rewarding politicians who say the right things and are adversarial toward the left but don't accomplish anything for limited government. In many cases, that will mean embracing candidates who are more polished and skilled. The problem with Todd Akin, who lost a Senate race in Missouri in 2012 that the Republicans should have won, wasn't his platform—it was his unpolished performance.

Republicans will also be told to be reasonable, to heed Obama's advice, and to give up on their resistance to tax increases. There may be some agreement in theory that would cut entitlement spending enough to justify giving ground on taxes, but nothing like that has been seriously offered yet, so it would be foolish to concede on an opening bid.

Instead, Republicans should move in the opposite direction: augment the Taxpayer Protection Pledge with anti-spending pledges. A new organization called the Coalition to Reduce Spending offers a good example. Their Reject the Debt pledge commits legislators to voting against unbalanced budgets and against increases in off-budget spending.

Republicans also need to think differently on other subjects. Defense is a constitutional responsibility of the federal government in a way that most priorities of the welfare state are not. But the GOP must scrutinize even legitimate spending as closely as they would examine funds going to liberal interest groups. Conservatives should not measure their commitment to national defense in dollars any more than they would so measure their commitment to education or health care. They must not trust the federal government with new powers they would not want liberal Democrats to exercise. And they must see that foreign policy can have unintended consequences that make us less safe, just as anti-poverty measures can hurt the poor and stimulus programs can damage the economy.

Attack corporate welfare. David Stockman advised Republican budget-cutters during the Reagan era to attack weak claims, not weak claimants. This is still good advice. This country wastes billions in corporate subsidies and distorts the free market. Conservatives' commitment to limited government is not an ideology of elite self-interest and disregard for the poor. Tax dollars should not be going toward General Electric, General Motors, Warren Buffett, or Solyndra. They are the welfare queens of the twenty-first century. It is time for the GOP to try what the journalist Tim Carney calls "free-market populism."

The growth of big government will create new political opportunities for conservatives and libertarians. Be prepared to seize them. The right's biggest gains have resulted from liberal excesses and misgovernment. Think about how to apply free-market solutions to pressing problems like health care. Ignoring the health-care issue is surrendering to big government.

The political journalist Ramesh Ponnuru warns against a mentality he calls "serve the check": "Make the middle class pay more of the price of government and it will demand less of it."[25] Conservatives should never be complicit in middle-class tax increases. But if liberals are responsible for such tax increases—and their appetite for government will inevitably force them to ask more of the middle class—they will inspire a revolt against statism. Trying to make big government affordable doesn't work. But the government's gobbling of middle-class incomes, in part through unlegislated tax increases such as inflation-induced bracket creep, soured the electorate on the liberalism of the 1960s and '70s.

Americans have been hostile toward activist government when said activism is seen as undermining middle-class values and interests. A good part of the Tea Party's initial appeal wasn't economic; it was cultural. We need to make the case that the looming entitlements crisis is detrimental morally as well as economically.

None of these strategies is guaranteed to succeed. The best time to act was back when Bill Clinton was pretending the era of big government was over. In the 1990s, the baby boomers were in their peak earning years; now they're retiring. The economy was growing smartly. There were Democrats as well as Republicans who thought fiscal stabilization was important, even in Congress.

The political conditions have changed and government has grown. Even if Barack Obama had never been elected, allowing federal spending to grow on autopilot after 2008 would have pushed us toward a full-blown, European-style welfare state. Big government has new clients, and we live in an era of economic uncertainty.

But we do know one thing: if we don't try, failure is inevitable. With the bill coming due, we cannot afford to fail. We must fight.

Big government has never looked so invincible. Yet it pays to remember an old saying: the bigger they are, the harder they fall.

ACKNOWLEDGMENTS

When I took on this project, I had no idea whether Barack Obama would still be president by the time it was published. Mitt Romney's campaign seemed listless. But just as I was trying to wrap things up, Romney turned in a strong first debate performance. The fiscal cliff also loomed, with no resolution in sight.

But I knew from experience that even electing a Republican president wouldn't mean the end of big government. Washington would be hatching new schemes and gobbling our paychecks either way. As it turned out, Obama was reelected, and he entered his second term with a promise to make big government even bigger.

Obama wants to prove false Bill Clinton's proclamation that the era of big government is over, and he's oblivious to Ronald Reagan's observation that government is often the problem rather than the solution.

I'm thankful to Marji Ross and Harry Crocker at Regnery Publishing for giving me the opportunity to write my first book, as well as for giving me the encouragement to see it through to fruition. Tom Spence was a talented and patient editor. Any defects are my doing, but many of the improvements and nice touches are his.

I owe thanks to Steve Martinovich of *Enter Stage Right* for giving me my first regular column for a national (as well as a Canadian!) audience.

I also am grateful to Scott McConnell and Kara Hopkins for giving me my first magazine job at the *American Conservative* and to current editor Daniel McCarthy for continuing to publish my work there.

I thank Bob Tyrrell, Wlady Pleszczynski, and Al Regnery for helping me continue my career in journalism at the *American Spectator*. I have greatly appreciated Wlady's friendship and counsel over nearly six years at the magazine, even though I still cannot spell his last name without the help of "cut" and "paste."

Finally, I thank Tucker Carlson and Neil Patel of the *Daily Caller* for putting up with me and supporting my work. It has been a great ride.

I write like a hermit, so I can't say anyone saw any chapters while I was working or even had much of an idea of what I was doing. But the book benefited from my many conversations with Jeremy Lott, Michael Brendan Dougherty, Jack Hunter, Katherine Ruddy, Philip Klein, and my old Ohio Wesleyan comrade-in-arms Brian Kirk, so they deserve some of the credit and none of the blame.

When I wanted to check half-remembered quotations from television talking heads touting big government, I almost invariably was able to find them preserved on the Media Research Center's News-busters site. I don't know how they do it, but I thank them.

I owe more than I can ever repay to my parents, even though they didn't like the calls to our home when I first started writing about politics while in high school, and to the rest of my family, who encouraged me to express my views even though they probably got tired of hearing them.

Thanks, as always, to my readers. Don't give up. Keep fighting.

NOTES

INTRODUCTION

1. Paul Krugman, "The Twinkie Manifesto," *New York Times*, November 18, 2012, http://www.nytimes.com/2012/11/19/opinion/krugman-the-twinkie-manifesto.html?_r=0.

2. Tom Coburn, "Senator Tom Coburn's Speech to the American Spectator's Annual Dinner," Senator Tom Coburn's website, http://www.coburn.senate.gov/public/index.cfm/rightnow?ContentRecord_id=09a88636-5f51-4b96-8aba-7229b85ce5f1.

CHAPTER ONE

1. "Transcript of second McCain, Obama debate," CNN, October 7, 2008, http://www.cnn.com/2008/POLITICS/10/07/presidential.debate.transcript/.

2.   "The Obama-Biden Plan," Change.gov, http://change.gov/agenda/
     taxes_agenda/.

3.   Peter Ferrara, "Barack Obama's Health Care Lies," *American
     Spectator*, October 15, 2008, http://spectator.org/archives/2008/10/15/
     barack-obamas-health-care-lies.

4.   Samuel Brown, William G. Gale, and Adam Looney, "On the
     Distributional Effects of Base-Broadening Income Tax Reform,"
     Brookings Institution, August 1, 2012, http://www.brookings.edu/
     research/papers/2012/08/01-tax-reform-brown-gale-looney.

5.   Rex Nutting, "Obama Spending Binge Never Happened,"
     MarketWatch, *Wall Street Journal*, May 22, 2012, http://articles.
     marketwatch.com/2012-05-22/commentary/31802270_1_spending-
     federal-budget-drunken-sailor.

6.   Tamara Keith, "Obama Fires Back on Spending Accusations,"
     National Public Radio, May 28, 2012, http://www.npr.
     org/2012/05/28/153860608/obama-fires-back-on-spending-
     accusations.

7.   Jennifer Bendery, "Jay Carney: Don't 'Buy Into the B.S.' from GOP
     About Obama's Spending Record," *Huffington Post*, May 23, 2012,
     http://www.huffingtonpost.com/2012/05/23/jay-carney-obama-
     spending-record_n_1539739.html.

8.   Devin Dwyer, "President Obama Denounces Republican 'Wild Debts':
     I'm Not An Overspender," Political Punch, ABC News, May 23, 2012,
     http://abcnews.go.com/blogs/politics/2012/05/president-obama-
     denounces-republican-wild-debts-im-not-an-over-spender/.

9.   Andrew Taylor, "Obama Off On Thrifty Spending Claim: Fact Check,"
     Huffington Post, May 26, 2012, http://www.huffingtonpost.
     com/2012/05/26/obama-spending-claim_n_1547737.html.

10. Glenn Kessler, "The Facts About the Growth of Spending Under
     Obama," Fact Checker, *Washington Post*, May 25, 2012, http://www.
     washingtonpost.com/blogs/fact-checker/post/the-facts-about-the-
     growth-of-spending-under-obama/2012/05/24/gJQAIJh6nU_blog.
     html.

11. Philip Klein, "The Man with the Plan," *American Spectator*, April 9, 2010, http://spectator.org/archives/2010/04/09/the-man-with-the-plan.

12. Robert P. Murphy, "The Fake History of the Depression," Ludwig von Mises Institute, April 20, 2009, http://mises.org/daily/3426/The-Fake-History-of-the-Depression.

13. Kenneth T. Walsh, "The Most Consequential Elections in History: Franklin Delano Roosevelt and the Election of 1932," *U.S. News & World Report*, September 10, 2008, http://www.usnews.com/news/articles/2008/09/10/the-most-consequential-elections-in-history-franklin-delano-roosevelt-and-the-election-of-1932.

14. "In Their Own Words: Obama on Reagan," *New York Times*, http://www.nytimes.com/ref/us/politics/21seelye-text.html.

15. Terence P. Jeffrey, "Obama: 'Since I've Been President, Spending Has Risen at Lowest Pace in Nearly 60 Years,'" CNS News, May 24, 2012, http://cnsnews.com/news/article/obama-i-ve-been-president-federal-spending-has-risen-lowest-pace-nearly-60-years.

16. Jonathan Weisman, "G.O.P. Balks at White House Plan on Fiscal Crisis," *New York Times*, November 29, 2012, http://www.nytimes.com/2012/11/30/us/politics/fiscal-talks-in-congress-seem-to-reach-impasse.html?_r=0.

17. Joe Weisenthal, "Tim Geithner's Solution to the Debt Ceiling Is So Reasonable, Nobody Could Possibly Object," *Business Insider*, November 29, 2012, http://www.businessinsider.com/tim-geithners-brilliant-solution-to-the-debt-ceiling-2012-11.

18. Rachel Weiner, "McConnell: Obama plan made me 'burst into laughter,' *Washington Post*, November 30, 2012, http://www.washingtonpost.com/blogs/post-politics/wp/2012/11/30/mcconnell-geithner-plan-made-me-laugh/.

CHAPTER TWO

1. George W. Bush, "The President's News Conference in Crawford, Texas," U.S. Government Printing Office, August 24, 2001, http://www.gpo.gov/fdsys/pkg/WCPD-2001-08-27/html/WCPD-2001-08-27-Pg1209.htm.

2.   Dan Balz, "One year later assessing Obama: Testing the promise of pragmatism," *Washington Post*, January 17, 2010, http://www.washingtonpost.com/wp-dyn/content/article/2010/01/16/AR2010011602950.html?hpid=topnews.

3.   David Wessel, "Everything You Wanted to Know About the Federal Budget But Were Afraid to Ask," *Wall Street Journal*, July 20, 2012, http://online.wsj.com/article/SB1000087239639044433090457753891008373424 8.html.

4.   CNN Political Unit, "CNN Poll: Americans Flunk Budget IQ Test," CNN, April 2, 2011, http://www.cnn.com/2011/POLITICS/04/01/americans.flunk.budget.iq/index.html.

5.   Barack Obama, "Remarks by the President in an AARP Tele-town Hall on Health Care Reform," The White House, July 28, 2009, http://www.whitehouse.gov/the_press_office/Remarks-by-the-President-in-AARP-Tele-Town-Hall-on-Health-Care-Reform.

6.   Bob Cesca, "Keep Your Goddamn Government Hands Off My Medicare!," *Huffington Post*, August 5, 2009, http://www.huffingtonpost.com/bob-cesca/get-your-goddamn-governme_b_252326.html.

7.   Kate Zernike and Megan Thee-Brenan, "Poll Finds Tea Party Backers Wealthier and More Educated," *New York Times*, April 14, 2010, http://www.nytimes.com/2010/04/15/us/politics/15poll.html.

8.   This quotation even appears on the Social Security Administration's website: Luther Gulick, "Memorandum re: Famous FDR Quote," Social Security, July 21, 2005, http://www.ssa.gov/history/Gulick.html.

9.   Susan Estrich, "The Mandate to Raise Taxes on the 'Rich,'" Creators.com, November 14, 2012, http://www.creators.com/opinion/susan-estrich/the-mandate-to-raise-taxes-on-the-rich.html.

10. Greg Mankiw, "A Master of Tax Avoidance," Greg Mankiw's Blog, November 26, 2012, http://gregmankiw.blogspot.com/2012/11/a-master-of-tax-avoidance.html.

11. David Corn, "SECRET VIDEO: Romney Tells Millionaire Donors What He REALLY Thinks of Obama Voters," *Mother Jones*, September 17, 2012, http://www.motherjones.com/politics/2012/09/secret-video-romney-private-fundraiser.

12. Craig Gilbert, "Paul Ryan on the Subject of 'Makers' and 'Takers,'" *Milwaukee Journal Sentinel*, September 18, 2012, http://www.jsonline.com/blogs/news/170242096.html.

13. Ginger Gibson, "GOP Returns Romney's 'Gifts,'" *Politico*, November 15, 2012, http://www.politico.com/news/stories/1112/83938.html.

14. Becket Adams, "Christ Christie Scrutinizes Romney's 'Gifts' Remarks," *The Blaze*, November 16, 2012, http://www.theblaze.com/stories/2012/11/16/you-cant-be-a-leader-be-divisive-chris-christie-scrutinizes-romneys-gifts-remarks/.

15. Ginger Gibson, "GOP Returns Romney's 'Gifts,'" *Politico*, November 15, 2012, http://www.politico.com/news/stories/1112/83938.html.

16. James Hoffman and Jonathan Martin, "Bobby Jindal rejects Mitt Romney's 'gifts' theory," *Politico*, November 14, 2012, http://www.politico.com/news/stories/1112/83892.html?hp=t3_3.

17. Pat Buchanan, "Mitt Wasn't All Wrong About 'Gifts,'" Creators.com, November 20, 2012, http://www.creators.com/opinion/pat-buchanan/mitt-wasn-t-all-wrong-about-gifts.html.

18. Aaron Blake, "The importance of 'gifts' to Latinos," *Washington Post*, November 15, 2012, http://www.washingtonpost.com/blogs/the-fix/wp/2012/11/15/the-importance-of-gifts-to-latinos/.

19. Stephen Dinan, "Data Shows Hispanics More Likely to Relate to Democrats," *Washington Times*, November 26, 2012, http://www.washingtontimes.com/news/2012/nov/26/data-show-hispanics-more-likely-to-relate-to-democ/?page=all.

20. Gregory Patin, "The Ron Paul Factor in the GOP's Defeat," *Washington Examiner*, November 10, 2012, http://www.dailypaul.com/262640/the-ron-paul-factor-in-the-gop-s-defeat.

21. John Gizzi, "Did Libertarian Party Cost GOP 9 Races?," *Human Events*, November 26, 2012, http://www.humanevents.com/2012/11/26/did-libertarian-party-cost-gop-9-races/.

CHAPTER THREE

1. Author's notes from event.

2. "Paul Ryan's keynote address at the *American Spectator*'s 2011 Robert L. Bartley Gala Dinner," Youtube video, November 1, 2011, http://www.youtube.com/watch?v=Lx-x_FVnRdQ.

3. Stephen Slivinski, *Buck Wild* (Nashville: Nelson Current, 2006), p. 141.

4. Jon Ward, "Paul Ryan Explains His Votes for TARP, bailouts, and tax on AIG bonuses," *Daily Caller*, February 14, 2010, http://dailycaller.com/2010/02/14/paul-ryan-explains-his-votes-for-tarp-auto-bailouts-and-tax-on-aig-bonuses/.

5. Ross Douthat, "Paul Ryan's Moment," *New York Times*, February 3, 2010, http://douthat.blogs.nytimes.com/2010/02/03/paul-ryans-moment/.

6. "Club for Growth Statement On The Ryan Budget," Club for Growth, March 21, 2012, http://www.clubforgrowth.org/perm/pr/?postID=1047.

7. Peter Suderman, "Paul Ryan: Radical or Sellout?," *Reason*, March 10, 2010, http://reason.org/news/printer/paul-ryan-radical-sellout.

8. Carl Hulse, "Senate Backs $318 Billion for Highways," *New York Times*, February 13, 2004, http://www.nytimes.com/2004/02/13/us/senate-backs-318-billion-for-highways.html.

9. Alana Goodman, "Romney Pounces on Santorum's 'Team Player' Blunder," *Commentary*, February 23, 2012, http://www.commentarymagazine.com/2012/02/23/romney-pounces-on-santorum-blunder/.

10. Ibid.

11. "Full Transcript CNN Western Republican Debate," CNN, October 18, 2011, http://archives.cnn.com/TRANSCRIPTS/1110/18/se.05.html.

12. CNN Political Unit, "Transcript of Wednesday's presidential debate," CNN, October 3, 2012, http://www.cnn.com/2012/10/03/politics/debate-transcript/index.html.

13. "Transcript And Audio: Vice Presidential Debate," National Public Radio, October 11, 2012, http://www.npr.org/2012/10/11/162754053/transcript-biden-ryan-vice-presidential-debate.

14. Slivinski, *Buck Wild* (Nashville: Nelson Current, 2006), p. 149.

15. W. James Antle III, "Bush Is Back," *American Conservative*, December 9, 2010, http://www.theamericanconservative.com/articles/bush-is-back/.

16. Michael Gerson, "No-bend Obama," *Washington Post*, January 27, 2011, http://www.washingtonpost.com/wp-dyn/content/article/2011/01/26/AR2011012606240.html.

17. Fred Barnes, "Big-Government Conservatism," *Wall Street Journal*, August 15, 2003, http://staging.weeklystandard.com/Content/Public/Articles/000/000/003/017wgfhc.asp.

18. Reihan Salam and Ross Douthat, "The Buck Starts Here," *Weekly Standard*, October 9, 2006, http://m.weeklystandard.com/Content/Public/Articles/000/000/012/762fiyke.asp.

19. "DeLay declares 'victory' in war on budget fat," *Washington Times*, September 14, 2005, http://www.washingtontimes.com/news/2005/sep/14/20050914-120153-3878r/?page=all.

CHAPTER FOUR

1. Rem Rieder, "A Skeptical View of the Cynicism Epidemic," *American Journalism Review*, June 1996, http://www.ajr.org/Article.asp?id=60.

2. Jeremy W. Peters, "Latest Word on the Trail? I Take It Back," *New York Times*, July 15, 2012, http://www.nytimes.com/2012/07/16/us/politics/latest-word-on-the-campaign-trail-i-take-it-back.html?pagewanted=all.

3. Mackenzie Weinger, "Tom Brokaw: White House Correspondents' Dinner Is Over the Top," *Politico*, May 7, 2012, http://www.politico.com/news/stories/0512/75992.html.

4. Jack Coleman, "Seize Them! Politicians Who Sign Norquist Pledge Are 'Traitors', Spews Bill Press," Newsbusters, November 28, 2012, http://newsbusters.org/blogs/jack-coleman/2012/11/28/seize-them-politicians-who-sign-norquist-pledge-are-traitors-spews-bil.

5. David Brooks and E. J. Dionne, "Week in Politics: Susan Rice and Fiscal Cliff," interview by Robert Siegel, National Public Radio video, November 30, 2012, http://www.npr.org/2012/11/30/166260515/week-in-politics-fiscal-cliff-and-susan-rice.

6. Brian Montopoli, "For Many Republicans, No Good Options on 'Fiscal Cliff,'" CBS News, November 28, 2012, http://www.cbsnews.com/8301-250_162-57555193/for-many-republicans-no-good-options-on-fiscal-cliff/.

7. "Cokie Roberts on Grover Norquist: 'The Emperor Has No Clothes,'" RealClearPolitics video, December 2, 2012, http://www.realclearpolitics.com/video/2012/12/02/cokie_roberts_on_grover_norquist_the_emperor_has_no_clothes.html.

8. "Norquist: 'Shame On' Peter King," Youtube video, November 26, 2012, http://www.youtube.com/watch?v=fszMNPVfCzE.

9. Frank Bruni, "Is Grover Finally Over?," New York Times, November 26, 2012, http://www.nytimes.com/2012/11/27/opinion/bruni-is-grover-norquists-hold-on-congress-finally-over.html.

10. Clay Waters, "New York Times: 'No Place in a Democracy' for Anti-Tax 'Purists' Like Grover Norquist," Newsbusters, November 27, 2012, http://newsbusters.org/blogs/clay-waters/2012/11/27/new-york-times-no-place-democracy-anti-tax-purists-grover-norquist.

11. Igor Volsky, "Republican Senator Rebukes Norquist: 'I'm Not Obligated on Pledge,'" Think Progress, November 26, 2012, http://thinkprogress.org/economy/2012/11/26/1233631/republican-senator-rebukes-norquist-im-not-obligated-on-the-pledge/.

12. Letter to the editor, Nashville Tennessean, November 30, 2012. See: "'Political courage'? Disavowal of pledge easy for Corker," Newark Advocate, November 30, 2012, http://beta.newarkadvocate.com/

article/DN/20121130/OPINION02/121129025/-Political-courage-Disavowal-pledge-easy-Corker.

13. Jeffrey Toobin, "Money Unlimited," *New Yorker*, May 21, 2012, http://www.newyorker.com/reporting/2012/05/21/120521fa_fact_toobin.

14. Howard Kurtz, "John Roberts Upholds Obamacare and Rises Above Partisanship," *Daily Beast*, June 28, 2012, http://www.thedailybeast.com/articles/2012/06/27/john-roberts-faces-historic-moment-of-truth-as-supreme-court-confronts-obamacare.html.

15. Jeffrey Toobin, "To Your Health," *New Yorker*, July 9, 2012, http://www.newyorker.com/talk/comment/2012/07/09/120709taco_talk_toobin.

16. David von Drehle, "John Roberts' Moment: The Chief Justice Weighs Image and Principle in the Obamacare Decision," *Time*, June 28, 2012, http://swampland.time.com/2012/06/28/john-roberts-moment-the-chief-justice-weighs-image-and-principle-in-obamacare-decision/.

17. David von Drehle, "Roberts Rules: What The Health Care Decision Means for the Country," *Time*, June 29, 2012, http://swampland.time.com/2012/06/29/roberts-rules-what-the-health-care-decision-means-for-the-country/.

18. "The Americans of the Year 2012," *Esquire*, December 2012, http://www.esquire.com/features/americans-2012/americans-of-year-1212-john-roberts#slide-6.

19. "Brave Thinkers," *The Atlantic*, December 2012, http://www.theatlantic.com/special-report/brave-thinkers-2012/.

20. "Liberal Man of the Year," *Wall Street Journal*, November 19, 2012, http://online.wsj.com/article/SB10001424127887323852904578129450389919028.html.

21. James Carney, "Hatching Mischief," *Time*, April 21, 1997, reprinted by CNN, http://www.cnn.com/ALLPOLITICS/1997/04/14/time/carney.html.

22. Robert Hendin, "As another government shutdown looms, is Washington having a 'deja vu' moment?," CBS News, February 23, 2011, http://www.cbsnews.com/8301-503544_162-20035440-503544.html.

23. "Budget Talks Fall Through," CNN, November 11, 1995, http://www. cnn.com/US/9511/debt_limit/11-10/debt_ceiling/index.html.

24. Richard O'Mara, "Are Orphanages Better for Kids than Welfare?," *Baltimore Sun*, November 27, 1994, http://articles.baltimoresun. com/1994-11-27/news/1994331010_1_orphanages-newt-gingrich-illegitimacy.

25. Elizabeth Drew, *Showdown: The Struggle Between the Gingrich Congress and the Clinton White House* (New York: Touchstone, 1996), p. 372.

26. Stephen Slivinski, *Buck Wild* (Nashville: Nelson Current, 2006), p. 74.

27. Timothy P. Carney, *Obamanomics*, (Washington, DC: Regnery, 2009), p. 72-74.

28. Jan Crawford, "Roberts Switched Views to Uphold Health Care Law," CBS News, July 1, 2012, http://www.cbsnews.com/8301-3460_162-57464549/roberts-switched-views-to-uphold-health-care-law/.

CHAPTER FIVE

1. William Saletan, "What Reagan Got Wrong," *Slate*, June 6, 2004, http://www.slate.com/articles/news_and_politics/ballot_box/2004/06/what_reagan_got_wrong.html.

2. Liz Neporent, "New York's Proposed Cap on Soda Size Gets People Fizzing," ABC News, July 24, 2012, http://abcnews.go.com/Health/nyc-mayor-michael-bloombergs-proposed-cap-soda-size/story?id=16848469.

3. David Frum, "Two Reviews," David's Frum's Diary, National Review Online, January 16, 2008, http://frum.nationalreview.com/post/?q=Z TkxMjUwNDYxNzRkYjkxMGFlMzIxMGIyYWRmNDI5YmE=.

4. Judith Graham, "Even A Small Slowdown in Obesity's Rise Would Save Big Money," National Public Radio, May 7, 2012, http://www.npr.org/blogs/health/2012/05/07/152184370/even-a-small-slowdown-in-obesitys-rise-would-save-big-money.

5. Paul Hsieh, "The Dangerous Synergy Between The Nanny State and Universal Health Care," *Forbes*, June 18, 2012, http://www.forbes.com/sites/realspin/2012/06/18/the-dangerous-synergy-between-the-nanny-state-and-universal-health-care/.

6. Liz Neporent, "New York's Proposed Cap on Soda Size Gets People Fizzing," ABC News, July 24, 2012, http://abcnews.go.com/Health/nyc-mayor-michael-bloombergs-proposed-cap-soda-size/story?id=16848469.

7. Anahad O'Connor, "The Not-So-Hidden Calories from Alcohol," *New York Times*, November 20, 2012, http://well.blogs.nytimes.com/2012/11/20/the-not-so-hidden-calories-from-alcohol/.

8. Liz Neporent, "New York's Proposed Cap on Soda Size Gets People Fizzing," ABC News, July 24, 2012, http://abcnews.go.com/Health/nyc-mayor-michael-bloombergs-proposed-cap-soda-size/story?id=16848469.

9. "Judiciary hearing on Elena Kagan, Dr. Coburn's Remarks (Day 2)," July 29, 2010, http://www.youtube.com/watch?v=Tgdetb9A4aY.

10. Josh Gerstein, "Kagan's Half-Answer on Eat Your Veggies Law," *Politico*, June 29, 2010, http://www.politico.com/blogs/joshgerstein/0610/Kagans_halfanswer_on_eatyourveggies_law.html.

11. Kathleen Sebelius, "A statement by U.S. Department of Health and Human Services Secretary Kathleen Sebelius," Department of Health and Human Services, January 20, 2012, http://www.hhs.gov/news/press/2012pres/01/20120120a.html.

12. "UNION OF ORTHODOX JEWISH CONGREGATIONS CRITIQUES ADMINISTRATION DENIAL OF EXPANDED EXEMPTION FOR RELIGIOUS ENTITIES' LIBERTIES IN HEALTH INSURANCE PLANS; CALLS ON CONGRESS TO REDRESS THROUGH LEGISLATION," Institute for Public Affairs, January 24, 2012, http://advocacy.ou.org/2012/union-of-orthodox-jewish-congregations-critiques-administration-denial-of-expanded-exemption-for-religious-

entities-liberties-in-health-insurance-plans-calls-on-congress-to-redress-through-legislat/.

13. Ross Douthat, "Defining Religious Liberty Down," *New York Times*, July 28, 2012, http://www.nytimes.com/2012/07/29/opinion/sunday/douthat-defining-religious-liberty-down.html?_r=0.

14. Yuval Levin, "The 'Compromise,'" National Review Online, February 10, 2012, http://www.nationalreview.com/corner/290763/compromise-yuval-levin.

15. William Saletan, "What Reagan Got Wrong," *Slate*, June 6, 2004, http://www.slate.com/articles/news_and_politics/ballot_box/2004/06/what_reagan_got_wrong.html.

16. Tibor Machan, "The Perils of Positive Rights," *The Freeman*, Foundation for Economic Education, April 1, 2001, http://www.fee.org/the_freeman/detail/the-perils-of-positive-rights/#axzz2IBJ9kHeY.

CHAPTER SIX

1. "Remarks by AFL-CIO President John Sweeney at AFL-CIO Post-Election Press Briefing," AFL-CIO, November 5, 2008, http://www.aflcio.org/Press-Room/Press-Releases/Remarks-by-AFL-CIO-President-John-Sweeney-AFL-CIO.

2. Jonathan D. Salant and Kim Chipman, "Labor Seeks Obama Help in Battle with Business Over Organizing," Bloomberg, November 8, 2008, http://www.bloomberg.com/apps/news?pid=20601071&sid=aiupc_xr1ZPE&refer=usgovernment.

3. Dan Morain, "A Union Challenge Lies Ahead," *Los Angeles Times*, November 16, 2008, http://articles.latimes.com/2008/nov/16/nation/na-unions16.

4. Patrick J. Buchanan, "Why Scott Walker Must Win," *Townhall*, March 1, 2011, http://townhall.com/columnists/patbuchanan/2011/03/01/why_scott_walker_must_win/page/full/.

5. Larry Sandler, "Milwaukee to See Net Gain from State Budget," *Milwaukee Journal Sentinel*, August 8, 2011, http://www.jsonline.com/news/statepolitics/127269673.html.

6. John McCormack, "Scott Walker's Collective Bargaining Bill is Working," *Weekly Standard*, August 8, 2011, http://www.weeklystandard.com/blogs/scott-walkers-collective-bargaining-bill-working_582151.html.

7. Jennifer M. Granholm, "Shaping America's Clean Energy Future," *Huffington Post*, September 14, 2010, http://www.huffingtonpost.com/jennifer-m-granholm/shaping-americas-clean-en_b_715822.html.

8. Tom Gantert, "Subsidized Green Energy Company Struggles, Lays Off Workers—Rewards Top Executives," *Michigan Capitol Confidential*, Mackinac Center for Public Policy, February 23, 2012, http://www.michigancapitolconfidential.com/16500.

9. Michael Bastasch, "Republicans Criticize Chinese Acquisition of Government-Backed Battery Maker," *Daily Caller*, December 11, 2012, http://dailycaller.com/2012/12/11/republicans-criticize-chinese-acquisition-of-government-backed-battery-maker/.

10. Peter Schweizer, *Throw Them All Out* (New York: Houghton Mifflin Harcourt Trade, 2011), p. 86.

11. Darren Samuelsohn, "Steve Spinner Leaves Center for American Progress," *Politico*, October 18, 2011, http://www.politico.com/news/stories/1011/66287.html.

12. Mark Hemingway, "Crony Capitalism: $737 Million Green Jobs Loan Given to Nancy Pelosi's Brother-in-Law," *Weekly Standard*, September 29, 2011, http://www.weeklystandard.com/blogs/crony-capitalism-737-million-green-jobs-loan-given-nancy-pelosis-brother-law_594593.html.

13. "Statement of Craig Witsoe Before the Subcommittee on Regulatory Affairs, Stimulus Oversight and Government Spending," U. S. House of Representatives Committee on Oversight and Government Reform, July 18, 2012, http://oversight.house.gov/wp-content/uploads/2012/07/Witsoe-Testimony.pdf.

14. Michael Bastasch, "Sources, documents suggest government-subsidized Abound Solar was selling faulty product," *Daily Caller*, October 2, 2012, http://dailycaller.com/2012/10/02/sources-documents-suggest-government-subsidized-abound-solar-was-selling-faulty-product/.

15.   Steven Raabe and Mark Jaffe, "Bankrupt Abound Solar of Colo. lives on as a political football," *Denver Post*, November 4, 2012, http://www.denverpost.com/business/ci_21918799/bankrupt-abound-solar-cololives-political-football.

16.   Bill McMorris, "Pat Stryker: Colorado Crony," *Washington Free Beacon*, October 16, 2012, http://freebeacon.com/democracy-alliance/pat-stryker-colorado-crony/.

17.   Michael Bastasch, "Sources, documents suggest government-subsidized Abound Solar was selling faulty product," *Daily Caller*, October 2, 2012, http://dailycaller.com/2012/10/02/sources-documents-suggest-government-subsidized-abound-solar-was-selling-faulty-product/.

18.   Carol D. Leonnig and Joe Stephens, "Federal Funds Flow to Clean-Energy Firms with Obama Administration Ties," *Washington Post*, February 14, 2012, http://articles.washingtonpost.com/2012-02-14/politics/35444143_1_clean-tech-clean-energy-investment-program-venture-firms.

19.   Timothy P. Carney, "Conservative money, bad; Liberal money, fine," *Washington Examiner*, June 25, 2012, http://washingtonexaminer.com/conservative-money-bad-liberal-money-fine/article/2500559.

20.   Robert F. Kennedy Jr., "Commentary: Obama's energy plan would create green gold rush," CNN, August 25, 2008, http://www.cnn.com/2008/POLITICS/08/25/kennedy.energy/.

21.   W. James Antle III, "It's Not Easy Being Green," *American Spectator*, April 24, 2009, http://spectator.org/archives/2009/04/24/its-not-easy-being-green.

22.   Larry Bell, "Obamacar: Bad Karma for Taxpayers," *Forbes*, September 25, 2012, http://www.forbes.com/sites/larrybell/2012/09/25/obamacar-bad-karma-for-taxpayers/.

23.   Robert Bryce, "America's Worst Wind-Energy Project," National Review Online, October 12, 2011, http://www.nationalreview.com/articles/279802/america-s-worst-wind-energy-project-robert-bryce.

24. W. James Antle III, "Solyndra Nation," *American Spectator*, April 25, 2012, http://spectator.org/archives/2012/04/25/solyndra-nation/print.

25. Editorial, "A Phony War on Crony Capitalism," *Wall Street Journal*, January 10, 2012, http://online.wsj.com/article/SB100014240529702 04124204577150424223893182.html.

CHAPTER SEVEN

1. Paul Krugman, "Why the Public Option Matters," The Conscience of a Liberal, *New York Times*, September 8, 2009, http://krugman.blogs. nytimes.com/2009/09/08/why-the-public-option-matters/.

2. Ibid.

3. "Epistemic closure and political disinformation," *The Economist*, May 5, 2010, http://www.economist.com/blogs/ democracyinamerica/2010/05/health-care_reform.

4. David Frum, "Waterloo," *Daily Beast*, June 28, 2012, http://www. thedailybeast.com/articles/2012/06/28/waterloo.html.

5. Peter Suderman, "Democrats Learned About ObamaCare's Individual Mandate From Watching the GOP," *Reason*, October 20, 2011, http:// reason.com/blog/2011/10/20/democrats-learned-about-obamac.

6. Avik Roy, "How the Heritage Foundation, a Conservative Think Tank, Promoted the Individual Mandate," *Forbes*, October 20, 2011, http://www.forbes.com/sites/aroy/2011/10/20/how-a-conservative-think-tank-invented-the-individual-mandate/.

7. James Taranto, "ObamaCare's Heritage," *Wall Street Journal*, October 19, 2011, http://online.wsj.com/article/SB10001424052970204618704576641190920152366.html.

8. James Carney, "Hatching Mischief," *Time*, April 21, 1997, http://www. cnn.com/ALLPOLITICS/1997/04/14/time/carney.html.

9. Timothy P. Carney, *Obamanomics* (Washington, DC: Regnery, 2009), p. 76.

10. Bruce Bartlett, "Republican Deficit Hypocrisy," *Forbes*, November 20, 2009, http://www.forbes.com/2009/11/19/

republican-budget-hypocrisy-health-care-opinions-columnists-bruce-bartlett.html.

11. W. James Antle III, "The Masscare Massacre," *American Spectator*, March 17, 2010, http://spectator.org/archives/2010/03/17/the-masscare-massacre.

12. Ibid.

13. "Massachusetts Patients Face Long Wait Times for Doctor Appointments," Kaiser Health News, May 9, 2011, http://www.kaiserhealthnews.org/daily-reports/2011/may/09/mass-wait-times.aspx.

14. Julie Rovner, "Emergency Room Doctors Say Health Law Will Make ER Crowding Worse," National Public Radio, April 28, 2011, http://www.npr.org/blogs/health/2011/04/28/135800784/emergency-room-doctors-say-health-law-will-make-er-crowding-worse.

15. Paul Krugman, "Why the Public Option Matters," The Conscience of a Liberal, *New York Times*, September 8, 2009, http://krugman.blogs.nytimes.com/2009/09/08/why-the-public-option-matters/.

16. Philip Klein, "If GOP continues to ignore health care, U.S. will end up with single payer," Beltway Confidential, *Washington Examiner*, November 29, 2012, http://washingtonexaminer.com/if-gop-continues-to-ignore-health-care-issue-well-end-up-with-single-payer/article/2514693#.UP4pY1HEH1U.

CHAPTER EIGHT

1. Peter Berkowitz, "Conservative Survival in a Progressive Age," *Wall Street Journal*, December 12, 2012, http://online.wsj.com/article/SB10001424127887324469304578144882157377760.html.

2. Charles Krauthammer, "Abortion: The Debate Is Over," *Washington Post*, December 4, 1992, A31.

3. Scott Galupo, "Don't Use the Obamacare Fight to Re-Litigate the New Deal," *U.S. News & World Report*, November 21, 2011, http://www.usnews.com/opinion/blogs/scott-galupo/2011/11/21/dont-use-the-obamacare-fight-to-relitigate-the-new-deal.

4. Krauthammer, "Abortion: The Debate Is Over," ii.

5. Ramesh Ponnuru, "Size Sense and Nonsense," *National Review*, February 25, 2005. http://www.nationalreview.com/articles/213773/ size-sense-an`d-nonsense/ramesh-ponnuru.

6. Nick Gillespie, "Q for Those in Favor of 'Balanced Approach' of Spending Cuts and Tax Hikes: How Many Times Has Real Spending Declined Since 1980?," *Reason*, November 26, 2012, http://reason. com/blog/2012/11/26/q-for-those-in-favor-of-balanced-approac.

7. David Frum, *What's Right*, (Random House of Canada, 1993), 25.

8. Charles D. Bloche, "AFL-CIO Chief Claims Reagan Budget Is Flawed," *Harvard Crimson*, March 10, 1981, http://www.thecrimson.com/ article/1981/3/10/afl-cio-chief-claims-reagan-budget-is/.

9. Richard J. Cattani, "Special-interest lobbies prepare to defend their 'turf,'" *Christian Science Monitor*, April 22, 1981, http://www. csmonitor.com/1981/0422/042239.html.

10. Stephen Slivinski, *Buck Wild* (Nashville: Nelson Current, 2006), 34.

11. Slivinski, *Buck Wild*, x, 33.

12. John Curtis Samples, *The Struggle to Limit Government* (Cato Institute, 2010), 142.

13. Elizabeth Drew, *Showdown: The Struggle Between the Gingrich Congress and the Clinton White House* (Touchstone, 1996), 128.

14. "Gingrich on Medicare," *New York Times*, July 20, 1996, http://www. nytimes.com/1996/07/20/us/politics-gingrich-on-medicare.html.

15. George F. Will, "String of broken promises results from diet high in pork," *Baltimore Sun*, August 8, 1999, http://articles.baltimoresun. com/1999-08-08/news/9908060196_1_cut-taxes-domestic-spending-human-capital.

16. Frum, *What's Right?*, vii, 26.

17. Frum, *What's Right?*, vii.

CHAPTER NINE

1. Interview with author.

2. Joshua Miller, "Scientist, Farmer Brings Tea Party Sensibility to House," *Roll Call*, December 22, 2012, http://www.rollcall.com/news/

scientist_farmer_brings_tea_party_sensibility_to_house-220306-1.
html?pg=2.

3.   Stephen Slivinski, *Buck Wild* (Nashville: Nelson Current, 2006), p.
      84–85.

4.   W. James Antle III, "Class War," *American Spectator*, May 2011, http://
      spectator.org/archives/2011/05/18/class-war.

5.   David Espo, "Possible Deal in Works As Shutdown Looms," *Time*, April
      8, 2011, http://www.time.com/time/politics/article/0,8599,2064188,00.
      html.

6.   Ben Feller, "Time's up: Obama and GOP scramble to halt shutdown,"
      Star Tribune, April 8, 2011, http://www.startribune.com/
      printarticle/?id=119391384.

7.   Alan Silverleib and Tom Cohen, "Obama: Progress made at night
      meeting, but no budget deal yet," CNN, April 7, 2011, http://www.cnn.
      com/2011/POLITICS/04/06/congress.budget/index.html.

8.   Paul Kane, Philip Rucker, and David A. Farenthold, "Government
      shutdown averted: Congress agrees to budget deal, stopgap funding,"
      Washington Post, April 8, 2011, http://www.washingtonpost.com/
      politics/reid-says-impasse-based-on-abortion-funding-boehner-
      denies-it/2011/04/08/AFO40U1C_story.html.

9.   Alan Silverleib, "Top conservative says no to budget deal," CNN, April
      12, 2011, http://www.cnn.com/2011/POLITICS/04/12/congress.budget/
      index.html.

10.   David Rogers, "CBO: Small 2011 payoff from big cuts," *Politico*, April
      13, 2011, http://www.politico.com/news/stories/0411/53098.html.

11.   Frank James, "How Washington Turned $38 Billion into $352
      Million," National Public Radio, April 14, 2011, http://www.npr.org/
      blogs/itsallpolitics/2011/04/14/135404502/how-washington-turned-
      38-billion-into-352-million.

12.   W. James Antle III, "Liberty's Maverick," *American Conservative*, May
      23, 2011, http://www.theamericanconservative.com/articles/libertys-
      maverick/.

13. Stephanie Condon and Brian Montopoli, "Congress passes spending bill averting shutdown," CBS News, April 14, 2011, http://www.cbsnews.com/8301-503544_162-20054026-503544.html.

14. Julie Hirschfeld Davis and Laura Litvan, "Obama Pushes for Debt Deal While Dismissing Republican Plan," Bloomberg Businessweek, July 17, 2011, http://www.businessweek.com/news/2011-07-17/obama-pushes-for-debt-deal-while-dismissing-republican-plan.html.

15. Rob Portman, "Make the Dollar-for-Dollar Rule Permanent," *Wall Street Journal*, August 4, 2011, http://online.wsj.com/article/SB10001424053111903341404576483791295988516.html.

16. "Obama: GOP Plan 'Doesn't Seem Like A Serious Plan To Me,'" RealClearPolitics video, July 15, 2011, http://www.realclearpolitics.com/video/2011/07/15/obama_gop_plan_doesnt_seem_like_a_serious_plan_to_me.html.

17. David Weigel, "Magic Words," *Slate*, July 22, 2011, http://www.slate.com/articles/news_and_politics/politics/2011/06/magic_words.html.

18. Candy Crowley, "'Cut, Cap, and Balance' Unlikely to End Debt Ceiling Struggle," CNN, July 18, 2011, http://www.cnn.com/2011/POLITICS/07/18/cut.cap.balance/index.html.

19. "House Approves 'Cut, Cap, and Balance' Plan," Fox News, July 19, 2011, http://www.foxnews.com/politics/2011/07/19/house-approves-cut-cap-and-balance-plan/.

20. David Jackson, "Obama-GOP debt deal skeptics include Bowles," *USA Today*, August 2, 2011, http://content.usatoday.com/communities/theoval/post/2011/08/obama-gop-deal-debt-has-many-skeptics/1#.UQApsFHEH1U.

21. Charlie Savage, "Senate Declines to Clarify the Rights of American Qaeda Suspects Arrested in the U.S.," *New York Times*, December 1, 2011, http://www.nytimes.com/2011/12/02/us/senate-declines-to-resolve-issue-of-american-qaeda-suspects-arrested-in-us.html?_r=0.

22. W. James Antle III, "Rand Paul, John McCain spar over NDAA 'indefinite detention' language," *Daily Caller*, December 19, 2012,

http://dailycaller.com/2012/12/19/rand-paul-john-mccain-spar-over-ndaa-indefinite-detention-language/.

23.　David K. Shipler, "Liberals Let Obama Get Away With Unconstitutional Actions," *Salon*, November 3, 2012, http://www.salon.com/2012/11/03/why_does_obama_get_a_pass_on_civil_liberties/.

CHAPTER TEN

1.　Alex Pappas, "Senate Prays for God to 'Save Us From Self-Inflicted Wounds,'" *Daily Caller*, December 30, 2012, http://dailycaller.com/2012/12/30/senate-chaplain-prays-for-god-to-save-us-from-self-inflicted-wounds/.

2.　Robert P. Murphy, "Sometimes You Should Look Up the Numbers, Fiscal 'Cliff' Edition," Free Advice, December 25, 2012, http://consultingbyrpm.com/blog/2012/12/sometimes-you-should-look-up-the-numbers-fiscal-cliff-edition.html.

3.　Thomas E. Woods, "I'm Just So Scared of the Fiscal Cliff," TomWoods.com, December 26, 2012, http://www.tomwoods.com/blog/im-just-so-scared-of-the-fiscal-cliff/.

4.　Suzy Khimm, "Obama Said the Sequester 'Will Not Happen. That Doesn't Change Anything," *Washington Post*, October 23, 2012, http://www.washingtonpost.com/blogs/wonkblog/wp/2012/10/23/obama-said-the-sequester-will-not-happen-that-doesnt-change-anything/.

5.　Jeremy Herb, "Under Pressure from Mitt Romney, Obama Says Military Sequester Won't Happen," *The Hill*, October 22, 2012, http://thehill.com/video/campaign/263425-obama-parries-romney-attacks-on-sequester.

6.　Timothy P. Roth, *Information, Ideology and Freedom: The Disenfranchised Electorate* (Lanham, MD: University Press of America, 1994), from foreword by Senator Phil Gramm.

7.　Rand Paul, author's notes from meeting.

8.　Steve Peoples, "Some Conservatives Would Rather Go Over the 'Cliff,'" *Chicago Sun-Times*, December 24, 2012, http://www.suntimes.com/news/nation/17214906-418/some-conservatives-would-rather-go-over-the-cliff.html.

9. Patrick O'Connor and Peter Nicholas, "How 'Cliff' Talks Hit the Wall," *Wall Street Journal*, December 21, 2012, http://online.wsj.com/article/SB10001424127887324731304578193770576333616.html?user=welcome&mg=id-wsj.

10. David Taintor, "Simpson and Bowles: Fiscal Cliff Deal 'Truly A Missed Opportunity,'" *Talking Points Memo*, January 2, 2013, http://livewire.talkingpointsmemo.com/entry/simpson-bowles-fiscal-cliff-deal-truly-missed-opportunity.

11. Sam Baker, "Simpson: 'Fiscal cliff' deal won't do 'anything really' to tackle deficit," *The Hill*, January 6, 2013, http://thehill.com/blogs/blog-briefing-room/news/275801-simpson-bowles-call-for-more-spending-cuts.

12. Megan McArdle, "Washington Goes Platinum," *Daily Beast*, January 8, 2013, http://www.thedailybeast.com/articles/2013/01/08/washington-goes-platinum.html.

13. Adam Liptak, "The 14th Amendment, the Debt Ceiling, and a Way Out," *New York Times*, July 24, 2011, http://www.nytimes.com/2011/07/25/us/politics/25legal.html?_r=0.

14. Nicholas Ballasy, "Democratic Rep: Debt-ceiling blank check is like Emancipation Proclamation," *Daily Caller*, January 4, 2013, http://dailycaller.com/2013/01/04/rep-davis-calls-for-confidence-in-the-president-with-debt-limit-control-video/.

15. Vince Coglianese, "White House Celebrates End of GOP Allegiance to Tax Pledge," *Daily Caller*, January 1, 2013, http://dailycaller.com/2013/01/01/white-house-celebrates-end-of-gop-allegiance-to-tax-pledge/.

16. Zeke Miller, "White House Claims Victory in Fiscal Deal," *BuzzFeed*, January 1, 2013, http://www.buzzfeed.com/zekejmiller/white-house-claims-victory-in-fiscal-deal.

17. "Durbin Open to Entitlement Reform, Says No to Touching Medicare Age and Social Security," RealClearPolitics, November 25, 2012, http://www.realclearpolitics.com/video/2012/11/25/durbin_open_to_entitlement_reform_says_no_to_touching_medicare_age__social_security.html.

18.   Robert Costa, "Out of the Coup, and Out of Sorts," *National Review Online*, January 10, 2013, http://www.nationalreview.com/articles/337317/out-coup-and-out-sorts-robert-costa.

19.   Cliff Asness, "We Are the 98 Percent," *The American*, January 7, 2013, http://www.american.com/archive/2013/january/we-are-the-98-percent.

20.   Patrick J. Buchanan, "How the Leviathan Ate the GOP," *American Conservative*, December 21, 2012, http://www.theamerican conservative.com/articles/how-leviathan-ate-the-gop/.

21.   Stephen Slivinski, *Buck Wild* (Nashville: Nelson Current, 2006), p. 87.

22.   Ibid., p. 87, and Tom Coburn, *Breach of Trust* (Nashville: Nelson Current, 2003), p. 72-80.

23.   Matt K. Lewis, "House GOP Freshmen Once Threatened Newt's Speakership Over Purge and Won," *Daily Caller*, December 6, 2012, http://dailycaller.com/2012/12/06/mark-neumann-urges-conservative-members-to-unite-behind-purged-colleagues/.

24.   Robert D. Novak, "Inside Report: Democratic Discipline, *RealClearPolitics*, December 13, 2007, http://www.realclearpolitics.com/articles/2007/01/inside_report_democratic_disci.html.

25.   Ramesh Ponnuru, "Starve the Beast, Protect the Middle Class," *Weekly Standard*, January 14, 2013, http://www.weeklystandard.com/articles/starve-beast_693765.html?nopager=1.

INDEX